Reading Grade 4

Table Of Contents

The student pages in this book have been specially prepared for reproduction on any standard copying machine.

Kelley Wingate products are available at fine educational supply stores throughout the U. S. and Canada.

Reading Comprehension CD-3711   Printed in the United States Of America   ISBN 0-88724-429-7

Estimating Reading Ability

The following graded word lists may be used to estimate a student's reading grade level.

1. Ask the student to read each word in the list.

2. Keep count of the number of words the student reads from the list.

3. Estimate the student's ability to read materials at the same grade level as the grade level of the word list. Base your estimate upon:

23 or more   The student can probably read at this grade level without help.

18 - 22   The student can probably read at this grade level if given some help.

17 or less   The student can probably not read at this grade level even if given help.

1.	amuse	13.	mission
2.	barefoot	14.	necessary
3.	builder	15.	operation
4.	colony	16.	postcard
5	crumb	17.	raincoat
6.	diamond	18.	rotten
7.	effort	19.	shovel
8.	fringe	20.	soccer
9.	gobble	21.	tender
10.	haunt	22.	troop
11.	insult	23.	uniform
12.	leash	24.	weekday
		25.	zero

Ready-To-Use Ideas and Activities

The activities in this book will help children master the basic skills necessary to become competent learners. Remember as you read through the activities listed below, as you go through this book, that all children learn at their own rate. Although repetition is important, it is critical that we never lose sight of the fact that it is equally important to build children's self-esteem and self-confidence if we want them to become successful learners as well as good citizens.

Story Comprehension

During or after story discussion, there are two different types of questions that you can ask to ensure and enhance reading comprehension. The first type of question is a factual question. This type of question includes question words such as: who, what, when, where, and why. It can also include questions like How old is the character?, Where does the character live?, What time was it when....?, or any question that has a clear answer. The other type of question is an open-ended question. These questions will not have a clear answer. They are based on opinions about the story, not on facts. An open-ended question can be something like: Why do you think the character acted as he did?, How do you think the character felt about her actions or the actions of others?, What do you think the character will do next?, or What other ways could this story have ended?.

Flashcard ideas

The back of this book has removable flash cards that will be great for use for basic skill and enrichment activities. Pull the flash cards out and either cut them apart or, if you have access to a paper cutter, use that to cut the flash cards apart. The following is just one of the ways you may wish to use these flashcards.

Reproduce the bingo sheet on the opposite page in this book, making enough to have one for each student. Hand them out to the students. Take the flashcards and write the words on the chalk board. Have the students choose 24 of the words and write them in any order on the empty spaces of their bingo cards, writing only one word in each space. When all students have finished their cards, take the flashcards and make them in to a deck. Call out the words one at a time. Any student who has a word that you call out should make an "X" through the word to cross it out. The student who crosses out five words in a row first (Horizontally, vertically, or diagonally) wins the game. To extend the game you can continue playing until you a student crosses out all of the words on his bingo sheet.

Vocabulary Bingo

		FREE		

3

What Are Symbols?

Symbols are drawings or letters that stand for something else. Right now you are reading symbols. Letters on this page stand for sounds that we use when speaking. When the letters are put together they are symbols for words that we speak. Symbols are full of meaning. They express, or tell, feelings about something. For example, every school has a symbol of their sports teams. Schools can choose tigers or lions as team symbols.   These animals symbolize, or stand for, strength and a fearless team. There are many symbols we use every day. The flag is a symbol of our country. Each television station uses a symbol so we can recognize, or identify who they are, at a glance. Restaurants have symbols. Even bathroom doors have symbols to help us recognize them. Symbols are an important part of our lives.

1. **What is the main idea of this story?**
    a. Symbols are drawings.
    b. Symbols help us recognize things.
    c. Symbols are an important part of our lives.
2. **What are symbols?**

_____

_____

3. **The word "express" means:**
    a. tell
    b. letter
    c. symbol
4. **What word means identify?**
    a. symbolize
    b. recognize
    c. express
5. **Why do schools pick symbols for their sports teams?**

_____

_____

6. **What does our flag symbolize?**

_____

THINK AHEAD: What are three symbols you see every day?

Phoenix

The phoenix bird is one of the oldest symbols that is still used today. Phoenix was the Greek name for a fictional, or make-believe, bird that was important to the sun god in ancient Egypt. The phoenix was a bird that looked like an eagle with red and gold feathers. The story is that the bird lived for 500 years. At the end of its life, the phoenix would build a big fire and burn itself to death. When the fire was gone, a new phoenix would rise from the ashes and begin its 500 years of life. The phoenix can be found in stories, religious ceremonies, and even government symbols. This bird symbolized the rising and setting of the sun. Later in history the phoenix became known as the symbol of death and resurrection, or life after death.

1. **What is the main idea of this story?**
    a. The phoenix bird is an ancient symbol that is still used.
    b. The phoenix is a bird.
    c. There are stories about the phoenix.
2. **What does the phoenix look like?**

_____

3. **What does "fictional" mean?**
    a. sun god
    b. not real
    c. eagle
4. **How many years does the phoenix live?**

_____

5. **What happens to the phoenix at the end of its life?**

_____

6. **What does "resurrection" mean?**
    a. make-believe
    b. symbols
    c. come to life after you have died

THINK AHEAD: Why might governments use the symbol of the phoenix?

Chrysanthemum

The chrysanthemum is a flower that is commonly called the "mum". It has been popular in Japan for many years. But there is one Japanese city, Himeji, that will not grow the mum. Those people think it is unlucky to even touch the mum. There is a legend in Himeji about a servant girl who lived a long time ago. The girl was named O-Kiku, which means Chrysanthemum Blossom. O-Kiku had the job of taking care of ten golden plates. One day she found that one of the plates was missing. She thought she would be blamed for taking the plate and that would bring dishonor, or shame, to her family. O-Kiku threw herself into a well and drowned. It is said that every night her ghost returns to count the plates. When the ghost gets to nine it screams and begins to count again. People of the city believe that the chrysanthemum is still unlucky, so they do not grow them.

1. **What is the main idea of this story?**
    a. One golden plate was missing.
    b. The chrysanthemum symbolizes bad luck.
    c. The Japanese like chrysanthemums.
2. **What are chrysanthemums?**

_____

3. **The name "O-Kiku" means:**
    a. chrysanthemum blossom
    b. flower
    c. shame
4. **What is the name of the city that will not grow mums?**

_____

5. **What is another word for "shame"?**
    a. mum
    b. O-Kiku
    c. dishonor
6. **What happened to O-Kiku?**

_____

_____

THINK AHEAD: As young children we sometimes think stepping on the cracks in the sidewalk is unlucky. What are some other things that we think are unlucky?

Crowns

Crowns are ornaments worn on the head to symbolize authority, or power. Kings and queens wore crowns. The earliest crowns are from ancient Egypt. Egypt had two kingdoms and each king wore a crown. When the two kingdoms united, or joined together, the crowns were also put together and made into a double crown. The double crown symbolized the joining of the two kingdoms. Ancient Greece had crowns but they were not for kings. Greek crowns were made of leaves and flowers and were worn by winners of sports contests! China had a kind of crown called the diadem. The diadem was a band of silk that was tied around the forehead. This band would often have fancy designs and jewels sewn on it. The tiara is a smaller kind of crown that is often worn by women. The crown given at beauty contests is a tiara. This crown is a metal band that has rows of stones or ornaments in the front. Crowns are symbols that everyone recognizes. They show that the wearer is an important person.

1. **What is the main idea of this story?**
    a. Kings and queens wear crowns.
    b. Crowns are symbols of power.
    c. Tiaras are types of crowns.
2. **What do crowns symbolize?**

_____

3. **What did the double crown of Egypt mean?**

_____

4. **The word "authority" means:**
    a. power
    b. crown
    c. diadem
5. **What is a diadem?**

_____

6. **Describe a tiara.**

_____

THINK AHEAD: Why do you think crowns were chosen as the symbol of kings and queens?

Heraldry

Knights wore suits of armor, metal that covered the body. When a knight was fully dressed in his armor it was difficult to tell who he was. Knights began to paint badges or symbols on their armor so they could be recognized easily.   Each knight picked a symbol that stood for who he was or what he was like. For example, a man named Oakes might choose an oak tree because it was a picture of his name. Other men chose beasts like the lion or eagle because they were brave and strong. Other symbols were simple bold designs because they were easy to recognize, even from a distance. These badges became known as a coat of arms, the symbol of a family name. People called heralds were experts who could easily identify any coat of arms. The custom of having a coat of arms can still be found in many parts of Europe and Asia and is known as heraldry.

1. **What is the main idea of this story?**
    a. It was hard to tell who each knight was.
    b. Heralds could read every coat of arms.
    c. Heraldry is a symbol for a family name.
2. **Why did knights need a coat of arms?**

_____

3. **The word "armor" means:**
    a. coat of arms
    b. a suit of metal
    c. experts
4. **How did a knight choose his coat of arms?**

_____

_____

5. **What is a coat of arms?**
    a. a symbol of a family name
    b. a coat made out of arms
    c. a trumpet
6. **What job did heralds do?**

_____

_____

THINK AHEAD: Design a coat of arms for your family name.

Eagle

Eagles are large birds that are powerful and brave hunters. Eagles can be found on every continent except Antarctica. They have been symbols of power and courage since ancient, or very old, times. Pictures of eagles can be found on ancient buildings in Egypt. Indians wore eagle feathers to show others that they were very brave. There used to be a lot of eagles, but they are becoming rare. They have been hunted and captured. They have also been killed by chemicals used to kill plants. One rare kind of eagle is the bald eagle. It is a large bird with a dark brown and a white head. The bald eagle is the national symbol of some countries. When people see the bald eagle they are reminded that it is powerful and brave. These countries see themselves like the eagle.

1. **What is the main idea of this story?**
   a. Eagles are birds.
   b. Eagles are symbols of bravery and power.
   c. The bald eagle is brown and white.
2. **Where do eagles live?**

_____

3. **The word "ancient" means:**
   a. long long ago
   b. brave
   c. powerful
4. **How do we know that eagles were symbols in ancient times?**

_____

_____

5. **What is a bald eagle?**

_____

6. **Why did the United States pick the bald eagle to be it's symbol?**

_____

_____

THINK AHEAD: Why do you think people like to hunt or capture eagles?

Flags

Flags are pieces of cloth that hang from poles, or something like a stick. We don't think of sticks and pieces of cloth as being very important. And yet, a flag is a very important symbol. A flag is a message that tells about a group of people. A white flag raised during a battle shows that one side is giving up. A flag placed on new land, like the moon, shows ownership. A flag flown over a city that has just been captured shows victory, or who won the battle. People fly the flags on certain days to show pride in their country. Each country has its own flag, kind of like its own coat of arms. Each flag is different and symbolizes what that country is about.

1. **What is the main idea of this story?**
    a. Flags are symbols of a whole group of people.
    b. The United States flag has stars and stripes.
    c. Flags send messages.
2. **What are flags?**

_____

_____

3. **Another word for "pole" is:**
    a. stick
    b. cloth
    c. flag
4. **Name three things that flags can tell us.**

_____

_____

5. **What does the word "represent" mean?**
    a. flag
    b. mean
    c. stand for
6. **Why does each country have its own flag?**

_____

_____

THINK AHEAD: Design a flag that could symbolize your whole classroom.

Statue of Liberty

When you think of a symbol of the United States the Statue of Liberty is one that pops to mind. The statue was a gift to the American people from the French. France gave it to the United States in 1876 to celebrate the first 100 years of being a country. The Statue of Liberty is a woman holding a tablet, or book, in one hand and a torch, or light in the other. She is 150 feet tall and stands in New York Harbor. The Statue of Liberty was the first thing many people saw when they came to this country. Her gentle face welcomed them and her light showed them the way to a new life. Liberty is thought to be a symbol of strength mixed with warmth, a sort of mother that protects her children. She represents what the United States means to a lot of people.

1. **What is the main idea of this story?**
   a. Many people have seen the Statue of Liberty.
   b. The Statue of Liberty is a female.
   c. The Statue of Liberty is one symbol of the United States.
2. **Who gave the Statue of Liberty to the United States?**

_____

3. **What is the Statue of Liberty?**

_____

4. **The word "tablet" means:**
   a. light
   b. book
   c. statue
5. **What does the statue symbolize?**

_____

_____

6. **How tall is the Statue of Liberty?**

_____

THINK AHEAD: Use the library to find out more about the Statue of Liberty. What is the tablet she is holding? Why does she have a crown on her head?

Liberty Bell

In 1753 the United States was not a country yet. It was still ruled by England. However, many people wanted to break away from England and become a new country. That year the Liberty Bell was made and hung in the Pennsylvania State House. On the bell was written, "Proclaim Liberty throughout all the Land". These words mean that liberty, or freedom, was what the American people wanted. In 1776 the Declaration of Independence was written and the Liberty Bell was rung on July 4th to celebrate. The bell was hidden during the war against England. It had become a symbol of freedom for the American people, and they did not want the English to take it away. In 1846 the bell was brought out of hiding to be rung once again. A tiny crack in the bell opened up and it could not be rung. The bell is still quiet, but it stands on display in Philadelphia as a symbol of the struggle, or fight, for freedom.

1. **What is the main idea of this story?**
   a. The Liberty Bell symbolizes the fight for freedom.
   b. The Liberty Bell is cracked and cannot ring.
   c. The Americans fought the English for freedom.

2. **In what year was the Liberty Bell made?**

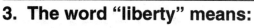

3. **The word "liberty" means:**
   a. country
   b. fight
   c. freedom

4. **What is written on the Liberty Bell?**

5. **Why was the Liberty Bell rung on July 4, 1776?**

6. **What is another word for "fight"?**
   a. struggle
   b. freedom
   c. liberty

THINK AHEAD: If the Liberty Bell had been captured by the English during the war, how would the American people have felt? Why?

Uncle Sam

Uncle Sam is a cartoon character who was first seen in the papers in 1812. The United States was fighting the British and many people were not happy about it. It was not proper, or right, to poke fun at the President, so someone made up Uncle Sam. Uncle Sam is a tall, thin man with long white hair and a beard. He is usually dressed in a coat covered with stars, striped pants, and a top hat with stars and stripes on it. He symbolized the politics, or government, of the United States. Uncle Sam became a way of poking fun at the government without naming any one person as the problem. During World War II, Uncle Sam became a good guy. He was put on posters and reminded people of how they could help the country during the war. Today Uncle Sam can still be found in political cartoons.

1. **What is the main idea of this story?**
    a. Uncle Sam is a symbol of the United States government.
    b. Uncle Sam is a cartoon character.
    c. Cartoons poke fun at the government.
2. **In what year did Uncle Sam first show up?**

_____

3. **The word "proper" means:**
    a. government
    b. correct or right
    c. politics
4. **What does Uncle Sam look like?**

_____

5. **What does Uncle Sam symbolize?**

_____

6. **When did Uncle Sam become a good symbol?**

_____

THINK AHEAD: Why is it all right to poke fun at a cartoon, but not a person in the government?

Peace Pipe

A peace pipe was a large pipe with a bowl for burning tobacco, a plant for smoking. They were usually made of clay, stone, or wood and were decorated in many ways. The Native Americans used peace pipes at meetings. The pipes were more than tools to smoke tobacco. They were symbols that meant a lot to the people who used them. Indians believed the smoke was a way to send messages to the spirit world, a way to ask for help with problems. When soldiers or traders came into camp the Indians might bring out the peace pipe. The two groups would sit down together in a circle. Each person took a puff and passed it around the circle. The pipe became a symbol of friendship among those who smoked it together. Peace pipes were strong symbols, thought to be charms with the power to unite people.

1. **What is the main idea of this story?**
     a. Peace pipes were a way to smoke tobacco.
     b. Native Americans used peace pipes.
     c. Peace pipes were symbols of friendship.
2. **What was a peace pipe used for?**

_____

3. **The word "tobacco" means:**
     a. a large pipe
     b. a plant that can be smoked
     c. a circle of friendship
4. **What did the Native Americans believe about smoke?**

_____

5. **How were peace pipes used?**

_____

_____

6. **If a Native American brought out a peace pipe, what did it mean?**

_____

_____

THINK AHEAD: What symbols do we use today to show that we want to be friendly?

Animals

Animals have often been used to symbolize special ideas. Knights chose to put lions on their armor to symbolize bravery. Chinese kings used the dragon to symbolize power. We still use animals to help describe, or tell about, how people behave. We say people are quiet as a mouse. People can be quick as a rabbit, low as a snake, or stubborn as a mule. Many times we are hungry as a bear or have the memory of an elephant. Sports teams also choose names of different animals to symbolize themselves. Falcons are smart birds that fly very fast. Dolphins are graceful and smart. Buffaloes are big and hard to move. Colts can run fast and avoid (stay away from) getting caught. Animals can be used to symbolize the many different ways that people behave.

1. **What is the main idea of this story?**
   a. Animals can symbolize how people behave.
   b. A dragon symbolizes power.
   c. Sports teams use animal names.
2. **What animal could we be as stubborn as?**

_____

3. **The word "describe" means:**
   a. to tell about
   b. stay away from
   c. graceful
4. **Why do sports teams often choose the name of a brave or fast animal?**

_____

5. **What word means "to stay away from"?**
   a. memory
   b. buffalo
   c. avoid
6. **What is a person like if he is described as a mouse, snake, or bear?**

_____

_____

THINK AHEAD: Can you think of three more animals that symbolize a human behavior?

Riddles

Twenty white horses upon a red hill.
Now they chomp. Now they stomp. Now they stand still.
What am I?

The words above make a riddle. It talks about white horses stomping and standing still. But riddles have a hidden meaning. Can you guess what the riddle is talking about? It is teeth! There are twenty white teeth in your mouth. The red hill is your gums. As you talk they move up and down as if they are chomping and stomping. When you finish talking they "stand still".   Riddles give a symbolic meaning to things. Riddles have been used for thousands of years. In ancient times wise people would often answer questions with a riddle. It was believed that knowledge was precious, or of great value, and should not be given to people who were not very smart. If a person could figure out a riddle, he was smart enough to know the answer.

1. **What is the main idea of this story?**
    a. Riddles were used as symbols.
    b. Riddles have been used for many years.
    c. Riddles are hard to figure out.
2. **What is a riddle?**

_____

_____

3. **The word "precious" means:**
    a. a lot of money
    b. meaning
    c. valuable
4. **How long have riddles been used?**

_____

5. **Why did wise people speak in riddles instead of giving an answer?**

_____

6. **What are teeth called in the riddle?**

_____

THINK AHEAD: Make up a riddle about something you have or use every day.

Birthstones

Each month of the year has its own special gemstone, or valuable stone. People who wear their birthstone are believed to have special luck. Birthstones date back to about 3250 years ago. Moses was the leader of the people of Israel. His brother, Aaron was a high priest. Aaron wore a breastplate, or armor for the chest, that had twelve stones on it. Each stone stood for one of the twelve tribes, or groups, of Israel.   Over the years the stones became symbols of the twelve months of the year. Each stone is thought to bring special luck. For example, the diamond is supposed to bring happiness. The pearl brings wealth or health. Here is a list of the birthstones for each month.

January - garnet	**February - amethyst**	**March - aquamarine**
April - diamond	**May - emerald**	**June - pearl**
July - ruby	**August - peridot**	**September - sapphire**
October - opal	**November - topaz**	**December - turquoise**

1. **What is the main idea of this story?**
    a. Birthstones are gemstones.
    b. Birthstones are symbols of good luck.
    c. Birthstones are over 3000 years old.
2. **What is a gemstone?**

_____

3. **What did the first twelve gemstones symbolize?**

_____

4. **Who wore the twelve gemstones on a breastplate:**
    a. Moses
    b. Aaron
    c. a priest
5. **What is a breastplate?**

_____

6. **Which birthstone is yours?**

_____

_____

THINK AHEAD: Use the library to find out what luck your birthstone is believed to bring.

Name _____

Colors

Colors are sometimes used to give meanings to things. When you see the color red, you think of things that are hot or dangerous. Fire engines are red so they can be easily seen and people will get out of their way. A red light or red sign on the street means to stop. Green is a color we use to mean "go". A green light on the street tells us it is safe to continue, or go on. Green signs in store windows mean the store is open. The color white can mean two things. If a white flag is held up it means surrender, or giving up. White can also mean that something is pure, or clean. Yellow or orange make people feel sunny, warm, or happy. Those are the colors used to symbolize the sun. Blue is a cool color, reminding us of water or ice. The use of colors help give meaning to things we see.

1. **What is the main idea of this story?**
   a. Colors can symbolize feelings or ideas.
   b. Red means stop.
   c. Blue is cold like ice.
2. **What messages do we get when we see the color red?**

   _____

3. **The word "continue" means:**
   a. stop
   b. go on
   c. be careful
4. **What two things can the color white mean?**

   _____

   _____

5. **What word means "to give up"?**
   a. surrender
   b. continue
   c. pure
6. **Why do the colors yellow or orange make us feel warm or happy?**

   _____

   _____

THINK AHEAD: What do some other colors (black, purple, brown) mean to you?

Producers

All living things will die without food. Food provides energy which is needed for growth and change. Animals must find food to eat. Plants do not need to look for food. They can make their own food by using energy from the sun. Plants have a special green chemical called chlorophyll that traps the sun's energy. The energy is used to make food from the water and minerals the plant gets through its roots. This process is called photosynthesis. Living things, like plants, that can make their own food are called producers. Living things that cannot produce their own food depend on producers. They need the producers to get energy. Cows and sheep eat grass to get their energy. People eat vegetables, fruits, and nuts to get some of their energy. Because producers can make their own food, they do not need to depend on other living things. All plants are producers.

1. **What is the main idea of this story?**
   a. Plants are producers.
   b. People eat plants.
   c. Chlorophyll traps energy from the sun.
2. **What are producers?**

_____

3. **The word depend means:**
   a. make food
   b. need
   c. get energy
4. **What is chlorophyll?**
   a. A process that changes energy to food
   b. The process of growing
   c. A green chemical that traps energy from the sun
5. **What is photosynthesis?**

_____

_____

6. **Why do other living things need producers?**

_____

_____

THINK AHEAD: What would happen if there were no producers?

Consumers

Animals need energy from food. They use the energy to grow and stay alive. Unlike plants, animals cannot make their own food. They must consume, or eat, food to get the energy they need. There are three kinds of consumers. Herbivores are animals that eat only plants. Cows, deer, goats, and mice are some herbivores. They eat the plants and get the energy the plant has stored from the sun. Another consumer is the carnivore. Carnivores are animals that eat only other animals. Lions, wolves, ferrets, and spiders are carnivores. They hunt or trap other animals and eat them to get their energy. The third type of consumer is the omnivore, which eats both plants and animals. Humans, bears, raccoons, and turtles are some omnivores.

1. **What is the main idea of this story?**
   a. Animals that cannot make their own food are consumers.
   b. Humans are consumers.
   c. Carnivores are consumers.
2. **What are the three types of consumers?**

_____

_____

3. **What word means "eat"?**
   a. carnivore
   b. energy
   c. consume
4. **What do herbivores eat?**

_____

5. **What type of consumer eats both plants and animals?**

_____

6. **What do carnivores eat?**

_____

THINK AHEAD: Find three pictures of animals that are eating. Identify them as herbivore, carnivore, or omnivore.

Food Chain

The sun shines down on the earth. In a pond the small plant, algae, gathers the sun's energy and grows. A water flea stops to eat some of the algae. The energy now passes from the plant to the water flea. The flea passes a frog who flicks his tongue and has the flea for lunch. The energy from the flea is passed on to the frog. Later in the day, a snake eats the frog. The energy is passed on to the snake. That night an owl swoops down and catches the snake for dinner. Once again, energy is transferred from one animal to another. This story shows how energy from the sun is passed on to larger and larger animals. As each animal hunts and eats, preys on, smaller animals they gather more energy. The passing on of energy from one living thing to another is called a food chain.

1. **What is the main idea of this story?**
   a. Animals eat each other.
   b. The food chain is how animals get energy.
   c. Living things need energy.
2. **What is algae?**

_____

3. **Where does a plant get its energy?**

_____

_____

4. **How does energy get from one living thing to another?**

_____

_____

5. **What does the word "transfer" mean?**
   a. to hunt and eat
   b. to pass on
   c. a small plant
6. **What is a food chain?**
   a. the things we eat
   b. the path of energy as is passes from one living thing to another
   c. a frog eating algae

THINK AHEAD: What did you eat for dinner last night? Pick one thing and trace your food chain back to the sun.

Scavengers

Some consumers do not catch or kill their food. They get their food from plants or animals that have already died. These animals are called scavengers. A hyena is a scavenger. It will wait while the lion eats what it kills. When the lion is finished the hyena moves in and takes what is left. Vultures are also scavengers. They circle in the sky and look for animals that have died. When no other animals are near, the vulture will land and pick at the remains. One scavenger that lives in the water is a crab. Crabs will eat the remains of dead fish they may find. Scavengers need energy, just like all living things but they do not prey on animals. They eat what is left from the hunt of other animals.

1. **What is the main idea of this story?**
    a. A hyena is a scavenger.
    b. Crabs eat dead fish.
    c. Scavengers eat animals that are already dead.
2. **Are scavengers producers or consumers?**

_____

3. **How does a hyena get its food?**

_____

4. **How does a vulture get its food?**

_____

5. **What are the three examples of scavengers given in the story?**

_____

_____

_____

6. **How do scavengers help nature?**

_____

_____

_____

THINK AHEAD: Name two other animals that are scavengers.

Parasites

Some animals get their food by living in or on other living things. These animals do not kill the animal they live on, but they may harm or irritate them. Animals that live on or in other animals are called parasites. A flea will live on a dog, cat, or other animal. The flea gets its food by sucking the other animal's blood. The dog or cat it lives on is called the host. The blood the flea takes is not enough to harm the host, but the flea causes the host to itch and be uncomfortable. Some worms are parasites. A tapeworm lives inside the body of animals. It gets its food from food the host has eaten. The tapeworm can take so much of the food (energy) that the host becomes very sick. There are even some plants that can be parasites. Mistletoe and some types of ferns live on trees, taking food and water from the them.

1. **What is the main idea of this story?**
   a. Parasites live on or in other living things.
   b. A flea is a parasite.
   c. Parasites can make the host sick.
2. **How does a flea get food?**

_____

3. **Where does a tapeworm live?**

_____

4. **What is a parasite?**

_____

5. **What does the word "host" mean?**
   a. an animal that lives on other living things
   b. the animal a parasite lives on
   c. mistletoe
6. **What kinds of plants can be parasites?**

_____

_____

THINK AHEAD: Find another example of a parasite.

Mutualism

Some living things have special relationships with each other. They help each other get food. A sea anemone will sting most fish, but it will not hurt a clown fish. When enemies are close, the clown fish will hide near the sea anemone and be protected. In turn, the clown fish drops some of its food which helps feed the sea anemone. The sea anemone and the hermit crab can also help each other. Sometimes the sea anemone will attach itself to the shell of the hermit crab. The sea anemone rides on the shell and has a greater chance of finding food. Often it will eat food that the hermit crab cannot finish. The sea anemone helps the crab, too. The crab is hidden, or camouflaged, so its enemies will not see it. In this way the crab and anemone help each other survive, or stay alive. This relationship of helping each other is called mutualism.

1. **What is the main idea of this story?**
   a. Clown fish help sea anemones.
   b. Crabs and sea anemones live together.
   c. When animals help each other the relationship is called mutualism.
2. **How does the sea anemone help the clown fish?**

_____

_____

3. **How does the clown fish help the sea anemone?**

_____

_____

4. **What is mutualism?**

_____

_____

5. **What does the word "camouflage" mean?**
   a. to hunt and eat
   b. to help each other
   c. to hide or disguise
6. **What does the word "survive" mean?**
   a. to stay alive
   b. a relationship
   c. sea anemone

THINK AHEAD: Can you find another example of mutualism?

Rocks

Rocks are everywhere we go. There are rocks in the dirt. There are small rocks, or pebbles, on beaches, in driveways, and on playgrounds. There are giant rocks in mountains and layers of rock under the dirt. What makes a rock? Rocks, like water, have a cycle, or pattern that repeats itself. Wind and water can break large rocks into small pieces no bigger than sand. These pieces are called sediment. Over time sediment gets pressed down in the ground and becomes layers of rock. As the rock gets pressed harder it can become heated by the core of the earth and will finally melt. The melted rock, called magma, can be pushed out of volcanoes. When magma reaches the surface of the earth it is called lava. The lava cools and becomes rock that will be broken down by the wind and water. This pattern is called the rock cycle.

1. What is the main idea of this story?
   a. Rocks change, and the pattern is called the rock cycle.
   b. Sediment gets pressed into layers of rock.
   c. There are rocks all around us.

2. What are pebbles?

_____

3. Sediment is :
   a. layers of rock
   b. small pieces of rock
   c. melted rock

4. What is lava?
   a. layers of rock
   b. small pieces of rock
   c. melted rock

5. In the rock cycle, what happens to sediment?

_____

_____

6. What causes rock to melt into magma?

_____

_____

THINK AHEAD: Draw a picture of the rock cycle.

Minerals

The earth is full of chemicals. Some chemicals that lay deep in the earth get pressed together to form a solid that we call minerals. Diamonds, emeralds, gold, and quartz are minerals. We can tell what the minerals are by looking at some of their characteristics: color, hardness, and shape. Minerals come in many colors. Pure quartz is white. Often other chemicals mix with quartz and give it a pink or black color. When the pink, white, and black quartz are rubbed against a special tile they all leave the same color. This color helps tell us the mineral is quartz. Other minerals will leave a different color that tells what they are. Minerals range from hard to soft. Some minerals can be scratched with a fingernail. Diamonds are so hard only another diamond can scratch them. Each mineral also has its own atom pattern, or shape. As a mineral grows, the atom pattern guides the shape the mineral will take. No matter how large or small the mineral is, the shape will always be the same.

1. **What is the main idea of this story?**
    a. Minerals are pressed chemicals.
    b. Minerals are identified by color, hardness, and shape.
    c. Diamonds and gold are minerals.
2. **Name four common minerals.**

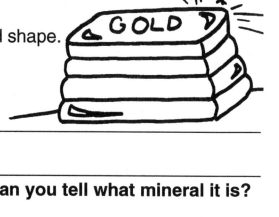

_____

_____

3. **Some minerals come in different colors. How can you tell what mineral it is?**

_____

4. **Are all minerals hard? Explain.**

_____

5. **How does a mineral get its shape?**

_____

_____

6. **What is a mineral?**

_____

THINK AHEAD: Put any six objects in a row. Arrange them from softest to hardest.

 CD-3711

Inside the Earth

What is inside the earth? Scientists believe the earth is a lot like a hard-boiled egg. The egg has a thin shell, a soft thick white layer, and a round yolk in the middle. The earth has a thin shell called the crust. It is about 8 to 32 kilometers deep. The crust is made of dirt, rocks, and minerals. Below the crust lies the mantle, a softer layer like the egg white. The mantle is much thicker than the crust and is very hot . The heat from this layer of the earth melts rocks that are at the bottom of the crust. The mantle is so hot that it pushes against the crust. Sometimes the melted rock pushes through the crust, causing volcanoes. No one has ever seen the mantle, but scientists learn about it by studying volcanoes and earthquakes. The very center of the earth, the part that is like the egg yolk, is called the core. Scientists believe that the core is about twice, or two times, as hot as the mantle. They think the core is made of the minerals nickel and iron.

1. **What is the main idea of this story?**
    a. The earth is shaped like an egg.
    b. Scientists believe the earth has three layers.
    c. The core of the earth is very hot.
2. **What is the earth's crust?**

_____

_____

3. **The mantle is:**
    a. hot melted rock
    b. the thin outer layer of the earth
    c. made of nickel and iron
4. **What layer of the earth causes volcanoes?**

_____

5. **The core is:**
    a. hot melted rock
    b. the thin outer layer of the earth
    c. made of nickel and iron
6. **Which layer of the earth is the hottest?**

_____

THINK AHEAD: Draw a diagram of the earth's three layers.

Name _____   skill: comprehension

Volcanoes

The earth's mantle is so hot it melts rocks. The melted rock is called magma.
Pressure inside the earth pushes the magma to the crust. Most of the time the magma
cools in the crust, turning into layers of hard rock. Sometimes the magma finds a
crack in the earth's crust. It pushes out of the opening and reaches the surface, or the
outside, of the earth. Magma that reaches the surface is called lava. When lava flows
from the crust it is called a volcano. If the lava has a lot of gas and water trapped in it,
it will erupt or explode out of the crack. Lava with only a little water and gas will not
erupt. This lava is thin and flows quietly from the cracks. As the lava cools it hardens
to form rocks. Sometimes the lava will pile up around the opening of the volcano. It
builds up to form a volcanic mountain.

1. **What is the main idea of this story?**
    a. Melted rock is called magma.
    b. Lava flows from volcanoes.
    c. Volcanoes are cracks in the earth where lava comes out.
2. **What is magma?**

_____

3. **What happens to most of the magma when it reaches the crust?**

_____

4. **What is lava?**
    a. magma that reaches the earth's surface
    b. a hard rock
    c. a crack in the earth's crust
5. **What does lava do when it erupts?**

_____

_____

6. **How are volcanic mountains formed?**

_____

_____

THINK AHEAD: Draw a picture of a volcano. Label the lava, magma,
and volcanic mountain.

Earthquakes

The inner layers of the earth are very hot. The heat causes pressure, pushing against the earth's crust. Cracks in the crust are called faults. Pressure from inside the earth can cause the crust along a fault to shift, or move.   When the crust moves, it causes vibrations (a quick movement forward and backward) that shake the surface of the earth. These vibrations are called earthquakes. There are many earthquakes every day, but they are are mild and we do not feel them. Sometimes earthquakes are very strong, shaking the earth so hard they can make buildings fall apart. Scientists measure earthquakes with a special machine called a seismograph.   The seismograph shows us how big the vibrations are. Scientists rate the movement on a scale from one to ten. "One" means the earthquake is mild. The stronger the earthquake, the higher the number. Keeping records of earthquakes helps scientists understand more about them.

1. **What is the main idea of this story?**
    a. Inside the earth is very hot.
    b. Movement of the earth's crust is called an earthquake.
    c. A seismograph measures earthquakes.
2. **Another word for a crack in the earth's crust is:**
    a. seismograph
    b. pressure
    c. fault
3. **What causes earthquakes?**

_____

_____

4. **What is a vibration?**

_____

5. **How do scientists measure and learn more about earthquakes?**

_____

6. **What do you know about an earthquake that is rated "one"?**

_____

THINK AHEAD: What do you think would happen in your city or town if a earthquake rated nine shook the earth?

How Air is Warmed

The earth is surrounded by a layer of air. This layer of air is called the atmosphere. In some places, like a desert, the air feels very warm. In other places, perhaps near a lake, the air feels cooler. What makes the air warm or cool? The sun warms the air, but not as you might think. You become warm when you sit in the sun. That is because you absorb, or take in, the heat from the sun. All objects on the earth absorb sunlight. Darker objects absorb more heat than light colored objects. Water does not absorb as much heat as land. Air does not absorb heat this way because it has no color and the sunlight passes right through it. Things that do absorb the sunlight become very warm and radiate, or give off some of the heat. Think about how it feels to stand next to an oven that has been turned on. The air near the oven feels warm. The heat from the oven radiates and warms the air near it. Air near cities is warmer because the buildings absorb and radiate a lot of heat. Air over water is cooler than air over land because water absorbs and radiates less heat than land.

1. **What is the main idea of this story?**
   a. Air surrounds the earth.
   b. Air is warmed by objects that radiate heat.
   c. Cities absorb a lot of heat.
2. **What is the atmosphere?**

_____

3. **How does air become warm?**

_____

4. **The word "absorb" means:**
   a. to take in
   b. to heat
   c. to give off
5. **What does the word "radiate" mean?**
   a. to take in
   b. to heat
   c. to give off
6. **Why is it cooler near an ocean than in a city?**

_____

THINK AHEAD: Why do you think water absorbs less heat than land?

Atmosphere

The earth is surrounded by a layer of air that we call the atmosphere. The atmosphere is made of a mixture of gases and small solid particles, or pieces of things (like dust). Oxygen and nitrogen are important gases in the air. All plants and animals need oxygen to live. Plants use nitrogen to make their food. Water vapor is another gas in the air. Water vapor is what makes much of our weather - rain and snow. Without this gas the earth would be too dry for plants to grow. Ozone is a gas that can be found in the top layers of the atmosphere. This gas screens out harmful rays of energy that come from the sun. We use air in other ways, too. Without air, birds and planes could not fly. We could not blow up balloons or bicycle tires without air. The atmosphere is very important to our lives.

1. **What is the main idea of this story?**
   a. Air helps us in many ways.
   b. Ozone keeps harmful energy away.
   c. Planes need air to fly.
2. **What is in the air we breathe?**

_____

_____

3. **The word "particle" means:**
   a. gases
   b. small pieces
   c. vapor
4. **What are the two gases plants and animals need to breathe?**

_____

5. **What gas protects the earth from harmful sun rays?**

_____

6. **How does water vapor affect the earth?**

_____

_____

THINK AHEAD: Make a list of six ways we use air.

Orbit of Planets

A planet is a large object that orbits, or moves around the sun. There are nine planets that orbit our sun. Mercury, Venus, Earth, and Mars are the four planets closest to the sun. They are called the rocky planets because they are made mostly of rock. The other five planets are called the frozen planets . They are farthest from the sun and are made mostly of gases. Jupiter, Saturn, Uranus, Neptune, and Pluto are the frozen planets. The farther from the sun, the longer it takes for the planet to orbit the sun. This chart show how long it takes each planet to orbit the sun just once.

Mercury	**88 days**
Venus	**225 days**
Earth	**365 days**
Mars	**2 years**
Jupiter	**12 years**
Saturn	**29 years**
Uranus	**84 years**
Neptune	**165 years**
Pluto	**248 years**

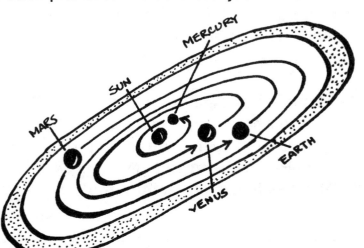

1. **What is the main idea of this story?**
   a. Some planets are made of rock.
   b. Frozen planets are farthest from the sun.
   c. There are nine planets that revolve around the sun.
2. **Name the rocky planets.**

_____

3. **Name the frozen planets.**

_____

4. **What does "revolve" mean?**
   a. made of gases
   b. move in a circle
   c. turn slowly
5. **How many years does it take for Jupiter to revolve around the sun?**

_____

6. **Why does Neptune take longer to revolve than Mars?**

_____

THINK AHEAD: Draw a picture of the sun and its nine planets. Label them.

Space Probes

We learn about planets by observing, or studying them. Scientists use a telescope to see planets. A telescope is a special instrument that makes far away objects look bigger. Some planets are too far away to see clearly, even when we use a telescope. How can we learn about these planets? Scientists send special spacecraft called probes into space. Probes travel through space, coming close to other planets. Telescopes and cameras are in the probe to record everything they see. Probes also carry special instruments to examine the weather and soil on other planets. The information is sent back to the earth where scientists can study it. The first probe, the Mariner 2, was launched in 1962. It gave us information about the planet Venus. Since then scientists have sent over 25 probes into space. Each probe tells us even more about the planets so far from our earth.

1. **What is the main idea of this story?**
   a. Probes tell us about other planets.
   b. Telescopes help us to see other planets.
   c. Mariner 2 was the first space probe.
2. **What is a telescope?**

_____

3. **What is a probe?**

_____

_____

4. **What information about other planets can a probe gather?**

_____

_____

5. **What does the word "observe" mean?**
   a. a special instrument
   b. to study
   c. probe
6. **What special equipment do probes carry?**

_____

THINK AHEAD: Why do scientists want to know more about other planets?

Holidays

The word holiday comes from "holy day" which is any day set aside to celebrate, or remember, something special. The holiday may be a time to remember independence or it may be a time to remember people important to our history. Some holidays are to celebrate religious events like Easter, Christmas, Yom Kippur, or Chanukah. Food is often a big part of holidays. We think of turkey with Thanksgiving, eggs and candy with Easter, and chocolate hearts with Valentine's Day. Some holidays, like Ash Wednesday and Yom Kippur, are celebrated by fasting, or not eating at all. Each holiday has special customs, or traditions, that go along with it. We watch parades and fireworks, give gifts and cards, eat too much or not at all, and play hard or just rest. Whatever holiday we celebrate, the most important thing we do is feel a sense of belonging as we share with others.

1. The main idea of this story is:
   a. Food is a part of every holiday.
   b. Holidays are a time for sharing and belonging.
   c. Valentine's Day is a holiday.

2. Where does the word "holiday" come from?

_____

_____

3. What does the word "fasting" mean?
   a. to go quickly
   b. to celebrate
   c. to not eat

4. What are some ways to celebrate holidays?

_____

5. What is the most important thing about all holidays?

_____

6. What is another word for "remember"?
   a. religious
   b. celebrate
   c. tradition

Think Ahead: On another piece of paper, list all the holidays you can remember.

Boxing Day

England celebrates a special holiday that is called Boxing Day. No, it does not have anything to do with a fight! Boxing Day is the first weekday after Christmas. If Christmas is on Tuesday, Wednesday is Boxing Day. If Christmas is on Friday, Saturday, or Sunday then Boxing Day will be on the next Monday. Now that you know when it is, let me tell you what it is! Boxing Day is a day set aside to thank people in service jobs. The English people gave gifts to mailmen, trash collectors, maids, or anyone who does jobs for them. But why did they call it Boxing Day? The name comes from the way the English prepare, or ready, the gifts. They are put into boxes before being wrapped up. Now you know about Boxing Day!

1. The main idea of this story is:
  a. Boxing Day honors service people.
  b. Presents are put into boxes then wrapped.
  c. Boxing Day is for mail carriers and maids.

2. In what country was Boxing Day first celebrated?

_____

3. What does the word "prepare" mean?
  a. to fight
  b. to ready
  c. to put in boxes

4. Who gets gifts on this holiday?

_____

5. When is Boxing Day celebrated?

_____

6. Why is this holiday called Boxing Day?

_____

_____

_____

Think Ahead: Why is it important to celebrate Boxing Day?

Australia Day

Australia Day is a holiday that honors Captain Arthur Phillip, the English founder of Sydney, the capital city. Captain Phillip came to Australia in 1788 to start a prison for England. One of the prisoners was an architect, who helped design the city. Sydney became a busy town that grew quickly. In 1890, Australia decided to set aside a day to honor their country. They decided on January 26 and called it Victoria Day, after Queen Victoria of England. In 1935 Australia changed the name to Australia Day. It is now celebrated on the Monday after January 6, and remembers Captain Phillip.

1. The main idea of this story is:
   a. Australia Day is a day to honor Australia.
   b. Captain Phillip founded Sydney.
   c. In 1935 Victoria Day was changed to Australia Day.

2. Why did Captain Phillip come to Australia?

_____

3. What does the word "architect" mean?
   a. prisoners
   b. a person who designs buildings
   c. the queen of England

4. When did Australia first set aside a day for their country?

_____

5. Why is Australia Day celebrated?

_____

Think Ahead: List all the holidays you can remember.

Groundhog Day

Each February 2nd many people want to know what the groundhog will do. A popular legend says that on February 2nd the groundhog comes out of his home. He has been hibernating, or sleeping there, all winter. If the day is sunny, he will see his shadow. The shadow scares him and he goes back into his hole. The groundhog will go back to sleep for six more weeks. That means that winter will stay for six more weeks! If February 2nd is a cloudy day the groundhog will not see his shadow. He will stay outside, meaning that spring has come. Folklore, or old stories, from Europe are much the same except the animal is usually a bear or badger.

1. The main idea of this story is:
    a. February 2nd is Groundhog Day.
    b. Legend says the groundhog tells us when spring arrives.
    c. Some people watch bears and badgers.

2. What does the groundhog do all winter?

_____

3. What does the word "hibernate" mean?
    a. come out of a winter home
    b. tell stories
    c. sleep all winter

4. What happens if the groundhog sees his shadow?

_____

5. What happens if February 2nd is a cloudy day?

_____

_____

6. What animals do Europeans watch on February 2nd?

_____

Think Ahead: On the back of this paper, list all the holidays you can remember.

Valentine's Day

In ancient Rome February 15th was a special day. Boys would pull girls names from a love urn, or large vase. They began to send cards to girls they liked the day before, February 14th. The cards were anonymous, they did not sign them, and the girls had to guess who sent the cards. Romans became Christians, a kind of religion, and the church did not like this custom. The church said the Roman boys had to stop giving the cards, but they did not stop. The church finally said they could send the cards if they celebrated the day as Saint Valentine's Day. Saint Valentine was a Roman priest in the church. The day was renamed and is now celebrated in many parts of the world.

1. **The main idea of this story is:**
    a. Valentine's Day is a day to celebrate love.
    b. Christians did not like the custom of giving cards.
    c. Valentine's Day is celebrated everywhere.
2. **What day was first celebrated by the Romans?**

_____

3. **What does the word "urn" mean?**
    a. to pull names
    b. a large vase
    c. to send cards
4. **Why was the day named Saint Valentine's Day?**

_____

_____

5. **What word means "not signed"?**
    a. urn
    b. valentine
    c. anonymous
6. **What day do we celebrate Saint Valentine's?**

_____

_____

_____

Think Ahead: Why do you think most valentines have hearts on them?

Memorial Day

The United States has set aside a day to remember people who have died while serving their country. These people were in the armed services: the Navy, Army, Marines, Air Force, or Coast Guard. Their job is to protect our country. Many of them died in wars. The holiday is meant for us to honor those people. Memorial Day was first observed, or celebrated, on May 30, 1868. The Civil War had just ended but many soldiers had died. People put flowers on the graves of the soldiers to honor them. Today almost every state celebrates this holiday on the last Monday in May.

1. The main idea of this story is:
   a. Memorial Day is to remember people who died in wars.
   b. People died to protect our country.
   c. Memorial Day is on May 30.
2. Who do we remember on Memorial Day?

_____

3. What does the word "observed" mean?
   a. to celebrate
   b. to do a job
   c. to end a war
4. What do people do on Memorial Day?

_____

_____

5. Name four parts of the armed services:

_____

_____

6. On what day do we celebrate Memorial Day?

_____

Think Ahead: What does your town do to celebrate Memorial Day?

Independence Day

July 4th is an important holiday for the United States. It is our Independence Day. On July 4, 1776 the United States declared, or stated, that we were a country on our own. We would no longer be a part of England. Independent means to take care of yourself without help from others. That is why July 4th is called Independence Day. Every 4th of July the United States celebrates the beginning of our own country. There are parades, speeches, and lots of fireworks.   People fly their flags to show they are proud of our country.

1. **The main idea of this story is:**
   a. The 4th of July is to celebrate the founding of our country.
   b. We have parades on the 4th of July.
   c. The 4th of July is for fireworks.
2. **On what day do we celebrate our independence?**

_____

3. **What word means "to state or say"?**
   a. declare
   b. celebrate
   c. fireworks
4. **What are some ways we celebrate Independence Day?**

_____

_____

5. **Who did the United States become independent from?**

_____

6. **What does the word "independent" mean?**
   a. holiday
   b. stated
   c. free and on your own

Think Ahead: What does your family do on the 4th of July?

Labor Day

Labor Day is a holiday that is celebrated everywhere in the United States. Labor means work. Labor Day is a day to celebrate the things we have worked for. We take a day off work and relax, or rest. It is a day to think about all the things we have worked hard to make or get. Most people take the day off and have fun. Europe began to celebrate workers on May 1. They call their holiday May Day. The United States and Canada celebrate their holiday on the first Monday in September.

1. **The main idea of this story is:**
   a. May Day is the same as Labor Day.
   b. People have fun on Labor Day.
   c. Labor Day is to celebrate what we have worked for.
2. **On what day do we celebrate Labor Day?**

_____

3. **What does the word "relax" mean?**
   a. think
   b. rest
   c. work
4. **What two countries celebrate Labor Day ?**

_____

5. **What does Europe call their labor day?**

_____

6. **When do Europeans celebrate their labor day?**

_____

Think Ahead: What is the date of Labor Day this year?

Halloween

Halloween has been celebrated for hundreds of years. People used to think that witches and warlocks, male witches, came out on the night of October 31. People would protect, or save, themselves by dressing in scary costumes and lighting big fires. They believed the witches would be frightened away by the bright light and ugly costumes. Most people do not believe that any more, but they still celebrate Halloween. It has become a holiday that children enjoy. On October 31 they dress in costumes and go trick-or-treating. After dark the children ring doorbells and people give them candy. People enjoy playing tricks and scaring everybody. Now it is done for fun, not protection.

1. **The main idea of this story is:**
   a. Halloween is a fun and scary holiday.
   b. Halloween is for witches.
   c. Children get candy.
2. **On what day do we celebrate Halloween?**

_____

3. **What does the word "protect" mean?**
   a. to ask for candy
   b. to keep yourself safe
   c. to scare people
4. **Why did people dress up and light fires on Halloween long ago?**

_____

5. **What is Halloween for now?**

_____

6. **What is another word for "male witch"?**
   a. Halloween
   b. protect
   c. warlock

Think Ahead: Draw a picture of the costume you will wear next Halloween.

Armistice Day

On November 11, 1918 World War I ended. The day was called Armistice Day. Armistice means a truce or agreement to stop fighting. In 1919 President Wilson said that Armistice Day would be celebrated to remember people who had died to protect their country. People who fought in wars are called veterans. Armistice Day would honor those veterans of the war. Every November 11 people fly flags and visit the graves of veterans. There are parades where veterans march so we can honor them. In 1954 the name Armistice Day was changed to Veterans Day. Now we honor the veterans from all the wars.

1. **The main idea of this story is:**
    a. Armistice Day was named by President Wilson.
    b. Armistice Day is to honor veterans of wars.
    c. November 11, 1918 World War I ended.
2. **What is Armistice Day?**

_____

_____

3. **What does the word "armistice" mean?**
    a. flags
    b. people who fought in wars
    c. a truce
4. **When was Armistice Day renamed?**

_____

5. **Who do we honor on Armistice Day?**

_____

6. **When do we celebrate Veterans Day?**

_____

_____

Think Ahead: Find out how many wars the United States has been in since 1918.

Thanksgiving

Thanksgiving is a holiday the United States celebrates on the fourth Thursday in November. It began in 1621 with the Pilgrims. They had come to America and had a very hard first year. Many people died because they were cold and did not have enough food. The second year they were here the Native Americans helped them. The Native Americans taught the Pilgrims how to grow corn and hunt for wild turkeys. That fall the Pilgrims had plenty of food to eat. They were very thankful. They celebrated their good year by praying and giving a big feast, or meal, that lasted three days. It was a time to thank the Indians for all their help. Many people kept the celebration every year. They give thanks for all the good things they have. In 1863, President Lincoln made Thanksgiving a national holiday, a holiday for the whole country.

1. **The main idea of this story is:**
    a. Thanksgiving is a time to celebrate what we are thankful for.
    b. Thanksgiving began in 1621.
    c. Thanksgiving is a time to eat a lot.
2. **Who started Thanksgiving?**

_____

3. **What does the word "feast" mean?**
    a. a big meal
    b. to be thankful
    c. Native Americans
4. **In what year was the first Thanksgiving?**

_____

5. **Why do people celebrate Thanksgiving today?**

_____

6. **What does "national holiday" mean?**
    a. a religious holiday
    b. celebrate each year
    c. a holiday for the country

Think Ahead: Why do you think food is such an important part of Thanksgiving?

Chanukah

Chanukah is a Jewish festival that is celebrated in December. It is also called the Festival of Lights. Chanukah is a celebration that began in 165 B.C. The Jewish people had been forbidden to use their temple, place of worship. They fought to get the temple back. It is said that when they went back to the temple they had only enough oil to burn their lamps for one day. A miracle, something impossible, happened and the oil lasted for eight days. During Chanukah one candle is lit each night for eight nights to remember the miracle. The eight candles are put in a candlestick called a Menorah. The Menorah has become a symbol, or sign of, Chanukah.

1. **The main idea of this story is:**
   a. Chanukah is a Jewish festival to remember a miracle.
   b. Eight candles are burned in December.
   c. The Menorah means it is Chanukah time.
2. **In what year did Chanukah begin?**

_____

3. **What does the word "temple" mean?**
   a. a place of worship
   b. something impossible
   c. a candle holder
4. **What miracle happened in the temple?**

_____

5. **What is a Menorah?**

_____

6. **What word means about the same as "symbol"?**
   a. impossible
   b. sign
   c. miracle

Think Ahead: Why do you think Chanukah is also called the Festival of Lights?

Christmas

Christmas is a religious holiday that is celebrated on December 25. It is a day set aside to remember the birth of Jesus Christ. In the year 274, the Roman emperor Aurelian declared this day to be the feast of the "Invincible Sun". Eastern churches picked January 6 as the day to celebrate because that is the day the three wise men reached Bethlehem, the city where Christ was born. Over time, the celebration became known as Epiphany and is celebrated from December 25 until January 6. This time is commonly called the Twelve Days. The four weeks before Christmas are called Advent. Advent used to be a quiet time to prepare for the feast of Christmas. During the last 100 years Christmas celebrations have slowly moved into Advent time. Christmas events now begin as early as Thanksgiving Day.

1. **The main idea of this story is:**
    a. Christmas is a religious holiday that is celebrated for many days.
    b. The Christmas holiday begins on Thanksgiving.
    c. Epiphany is another name for Christmas.

2. **In what year was Christmas first celebrated?**

_____

3. **What is another name for "Epiphany"?**
    a. Advent
    b. the Twelve Days
    c. Aurelian

4. **What was Christmas called when it first began?**

_____

5. **What Roman emperor began the celebration?**

_____

6. **What is "Advent" ?**
    a. a religious holiday
    b. the Twelve Days of Christmas
    c. the four weeks before Christmas

Think Ahead: Why do you think the celebration of Christmas has slowly moved up to right after Thanksgiving?

Honoring Others

There are many holidays that are celebrated quietly. The country does not stop work to celebrate and there are no parades. These days are set aside to remember special groups of people. Secretaries are remembered on the last Wednesday in April. Mother's Day is the first Sunday in May. Father's Day is the third Sunday in June. Friendship Day is in August. A day to honor Grandparents is the second Sunday in September. On the third Saturday of October we honor those we love and call it Sweetest Day. These holidays are called civil holidays, days that the country remembers but does not make a big fuss over. On civil holidays we send cards, call people, and do nice things for those we are honoring.

1. **The main idea of this story is:**
   a. Mother's Day is in May.
   b. Everyone works on civil holidays.
   c. Civil holidays are days that we honor other people.

2. **When do we celebrate Father's Day?**

   _____

3. **List three civil holidays we celebrate.**

   _____

   _____

   _____

4. **On what day do we celebrate Grandparents Day?**

   _____

5. **What month do we celebrate our friendships?**

   _____

6. **What are some of the ways we celebrate civil holidays?**

   _____

   _____

Think Ahead: What does your family do to celebrate civil holidays?

Greeting Cards

A greeting card is a printed message, or thought, that we send to other people. There is usually a picture on the front and the message inside the card. The custom of sending greeting cards can be traced back to about 500 B.C. when Egyptians sent written messages with their New Year's gifts. Greeting cards also played an important part in the holiday of Valentine's Day when people would send messages to their sweethearts. The first printed cards were found in Europe in the 1400's. People made woodcut prints, a design cut out of wood then painted and stamped on paper. Europeans sent these cards as New Year's greetings. The modern greeting card became popular in the late 1800's because printing was quick and easy and cards could be mailed to people across the country. Today greeting cards can be found for civil and religious holidays, anniversaries, birthdays, and just about any occasion you can think of.

1. **The main idea of this story is:**
   a. Greeting cards have been around for over two thousand years.
   b. Greeting cards are a way of sending messages for special occasions.
   c. We send greeting cards on birthdays.
2. **What does the word "message" mean?**
   a. a greeting card
   b. a printed thought or feeling
   c. New Years gifts
3. **When did people first send greeting cards to others?**

_____

4. **Where were the first printed greeting cards found?**

_____

5. **How were the first printed greeting cards made?**

_____

6. **Why did cards become popular in the late 1800's?**

_____

_____

Think Ahead: On what occasions does your family exchange greeting cards?

Nouns

Cloze is a reading exercise where some of the words are missing and you must put them back in. Read the story below. Some of the nouns have been taken out. Fill in the blanks with the words below the story.

Caitlin's Big Day

Caitlin counted her money one last time. It was all there. _____ had saved her extra _____ for the last five weeks. She had planned this day for a long _____ and now it was here! Caitlin carefully put the money in her _____. She did not want to lose a single_____. Caitlin walked to Lee's house. Lee had saved her money, too. The _____ walked to town. They went to the movie theater and bought two _____ for the show. Each girl bought a box of _____ and a cold _____. They watched the _____, enjoying every minute of it. When the movie was over, Caitlin and Lee walked to the ice cream _____. They had just enough money left for a hot fudge _____. What a wonderful _____ it had been!

**Caitlin   day   girls   money   movie   penny   popcorn
soda   store   sundae   tickets   time   wallet**

Nouns

Cloze is a reading exercise where some of the words are missing and you must put them back in. Read the story below. Some of the nouns have been taken out. Fill in the blanks with the words below the story.

The Parade

Ryan and Evan were excited. _____ they

were going to the _____ parade. The circus

came to _____ every five years. The last

_____ it was here Ryan and Evan

had the _____ and could not go. This

time _____ were healthy and eager to see

everything! Ryan had asked his father what kinds of

_____ they would see. Evan asked his

mother to tell _____ about the circus acts. He

wanted to know all about the dancing _____ and

tightrope walkers. Both _____ had their cameras

so they could take _____ of the things they liked best.

Ryan and Evan were all dressed and ready to go. There was only one

_____ . The _____

would not begin for three more _____ !

**animals bears boys circus him hours measles
parade pictures problem they time Today town**

Nouns

Cloze is a reading exercise where some of the words are missing and you must put them back in. Read the story below. Some of the nouns have been taken out. Fill in the blanks with the words below the story.

A Visitor

The teacher told the children to clear their desks. She had

_____ important to

tell _____ . The class buzzed

with _____ as books

and _____ were quickly stuffed into

desks. They could tell that the _____

was excited and happy. Her cheeks glowed and her eyes sparkled as

_____ watched them get ready.

The _____ were finished in no time.

They sat with their _____ folded on their

laps or desktops. Every _____ was fixed

on the teacher. What could be so important? The teacher cleared her

_____ and began. The class had an important

_____ who was waiting in the

_____ . The _____

opened and in stepped a _____ dressed in a suit.

It was the _____ of their country! The class

gasped in surprise.

children   door   eye   hall   hands   man   pencils   leader
she   something   teacher   them   throat   visitor   whispers

Verbs

Cloze is a reading exercise where some of the words are missing and you must put them back in. Read the story below. Some of the verbs have been taken out. Fill in the blanks with the words below the story.

A Paper Route

John has a job. Early each morning he _____ up

and quickly _____ . He must be out of the house

and on the job by five o'clock. John _____ papers

to the people in his neighborhood. He _____ at

the drugstore just in time to meet the paper truck. He must

_____ out 72 papers for his route. John

carefully _____ each paper and

_____ it into a plastic bag. When all his

papers _____ ready, John

_____ them into the basket on his bicycle.

Now the real work begins! John _____ his bike

through the neighborhood. He _____ papers on

front lawns or porches. John _____ careful to

leave the paper where the customer _____ to find

it. John _____ good when he is

_____ his job. He _____

that his job is important to many people.

are   arrives   count   delivers   doing   dresses   feels   folds
gets   is   knows   likes   loads   pedals   slides   tosses

Verbs

Cloze is a reading exercise where some of the words are missing and you must put them back in. Read the story below. Some of the verbs have been taken out. Fill in the blanks with the words below the story.

Nosy the Kitten

Nosy was a happy little kitten. She _____ a

mother who _____ her very much. She

_____ in a warm house with many children.

Nosy had everything a kitten could _____ . The

only problem _____ that Nosy was nosy! Just

last week she had _____ with a ball of yarn and

got all _____ up in it. One of the children

_____ almost half an hour

_____ the yarn from her paws. This morning

Nosy _____ a nest near the top of the maple tree.

She _____ up the tree to

_____ what was in the nest. It was not

hard to _____ the high limb.

_____ down was not so easy. Nosy

_____ down from the high branch and

became dizzy. Now she is _____ in the tree.
What a nosy kitten!

climbed had Getting lived looked loved played reach
saw see spent stuck tangled unwrapping want was

Name _____

Verbs

Cloze is a reading exercise where some of the words are missing and you must put them back in. Read the story below. Some of the verbs have been taken out. Fill in the blanks with the words below the story.

The Hungry Bear

Betsy bear was taking her winter nap in her den. She felt water

_____ on her nose. Drip. Drip. Drip. Betsy

lazily _____ one eye and

_____ up. The winter snow was

_____ . It was time to get up. Betsy

_____ her huge paws over her head.

She _____ a big yawn and sighed. It was

so cozy in her den. She really didn't want to _____

up yet. Maybe she could _____ over and go back to

_____ for just a little while. Betsy settled back down

and _____ her eyes. Suddenly she heard a loud

_____ noise. Was that another bear? Betsy

_____ up and looked around. There

_____ the noise again. She looked down

at her tummy. The growl had _____ from her!

Betsy's tummy _____ it was time to get up and

_____ something to eat. Spring had arrived!

**closed come dripping find growling knew looked melting
opened roll sat sleep stretched wake was yawned**

Adjectives

Clozo ic a reading exercise where some of the words are missing and you must put them back in. Read the story below. Some of the adjectives have been taken out. Fill in the blanks with the words below the story.

The Parrot

Sam knew just what he wanted for his birthday. Last week he had

gone to _____ pet store to look at the

_____ puppies in the _____

window. Sam loved to rub their _____ ears and feel

their _____ noses. But as he entered the store

Sam heard a _____ squawk. Sam saw a

_____ wire cage near the back of the store.

Inside the cage was the _____ bird he had ever

seen. Mr. Brown told Sam that the bird was a parrot.   The parrot had green and

_____ feathers, a _____

beak, and _____ claws on each toe. The

_____ bird looked at Sam and said, "Hello boy."

Sam laughed and petted the bird's _____ feathers.

He knew that the _____ bird was the

_____ gift for him. That is what he wanted

for his birthday!

beautiful   big   cute   front   furry   hooked   large   loud
Mr. Brown's   perfect   prettiest   sharp   soft   wet   yellow

Adjectives

Cloze is a reading exercise where some of the words are missing and you must put them back in. Read the story below. Some of the adjectives have been taken out. Fill in the blanks with the words below the story.

The Farm

Brandon had a great time last summer. He had spent

_____ weeks on his uncle's farm. Brandon

lived in a _____ city, so the farm was

_____ and different for him. Every

morning the _____ rooster stood on

the _____ fence rail and crowed at the

_____ sun. Brandon had

_____ chores to do before breakfast.

He gathered the _____ eggs the hens had

just laid. He gently reached under each _____

hen and carefully lifted out the _____ eggs.

Then it was time to feed the _____ sheep. After

that it was time to give the horses _____ water to

drink. Finally Brandon went back to the kitchen where he found

_____ bacon and _____

eggs waiting for him. He was _____ hungry and

_____ ate a lot for breakfast. Life on the farm was

lots of fun!

**always big brown clean crisp fat glowing many new old
scrambled two very warm wooden woolly**

Adjectives

Cloze is a reading exercise where some of the words are missing and you must put them back in. Read the story below. Some of the adjectives have been taken out. Fill in the blanks with the words below the story.

A Great Meal

This Thanksgiving I had the best meal ever! My mother baked a

_____ pound turkey. The skin was a

golden _____ color. The meat was so

_____ I had to use two napkins to keep

my chin dry! The red _____ sauce was

just _____ enough for me. My sister liked the

_____ potatoes, but I liked the yams with

_____ marshmallows on top. We had a jello

salad that sat on _____ lettuce leaves.

The _____ rolls tasted so good I ate

_____ of them! But my favorite food was

the _____ pie with _____

cream on top. I felt so full I could barely walk. After that

_____ meal, I found

a_____ pillow and laid down. We watched a

_____ game and I fell _____

asleep. What a wonderful day!

**brown   comfortable   cranberry   delicious   fast   fifteen   football
four   green   hot   juicy   mashed   melted   pumpkin   sweet   whipped**

Cloze

Cloze is a reading exercise where some of the words are missing and you must put them back in. Read the story below. Every tenth word has been taken out. Fill in the blanks with the words you think will make sense.

A Popcorn Ball

My father took me to a baseball game today. The stands were crowded but
we found our seats. _____ was upset because
we were almost at the end _____ the stands. They
were not good seats. I didn't _____ . I liked being
with my dad, even if we _____ not see the game
very well. Dad settled down _____ bought each of
us a box of popcorn. The _____ was stale and cost
too much money. Poor Dad _____ not having a
very good day. The first batter _____ the ball. The
ball popped into the air _____ was coming into the
stands. It was a home _____ ! Dad stood up and
the ball landed in his _____ of popcorn. The popcorn
and seats turned out to be pretty good after all!

and   and   box   could   Dad   hit   mind   of   popcorn   run   was

Cloze

Cloze is a reading exercise where some of the words are missing and you must put them back in. Read the story below. Every tenth word has been taken out. Fill in the blanks with the words you think will make sense.

The Haunted House

It was a very dark night. The house looked scary standing under the

shadowy old _____ trees. The four friends

stood at the front gate. _____ one wanted to

be the first to step into _____ yard. One of them

pointed a flashlight at the _____ windows. They

looked dusty and several of them were _____. The

house sure looked haunted, even though none of _____

believed that it was. Not one of the boys _____ a

word. Each boy was frightened but did not _____ the

others to know. An owl hooted from the _____ of the

largest oak tree. The boys all jumped ,_____ did not

run away. The tallest boy cleared his _____ but did not

speak. Were they really going to go into that spooky old place?

broken   but   dark   No   oak   said   the   them   throat   top   want

Cloze

Cloze is a reading exercise where some of the words are missing and you must put them back in. Read the story below. Every eighth word has been taken out. Fill in the blanks with the words you think will make sense.

Hunting For a Rainbow

Maggie pulled the rubber boots on over her shoes. She slid into

her yellow raincoat and _____ the front closed.

This was just the _____ she had been hoping for.

The sky _____ a light grey with bits of blue

_____ through. Maggie knew that this time

she _____ find what she was looking for. She

_____ out the door and opened the big

_____ umbrella over her head. The light

rain _____ on the rounded top and quickly

slid _____ the sides. Her boots splashed

through the _____ as Maggie walked through

them. The rain _____ almost stopped so Maggie

hurried faster. She _____ the top of the hill and

looked. _____ enough, this time she had found it!

Beyond the hill was a beautiful rainbow sparkling in the sun.

**danced down had peeking puddles reached red
snapped stepped Sure was weather would**

Cloze

Cloze is a reading exercise where some of the words are missing and you must put them back in. Read the story below. Every eighth word has been taken out. Fill in the blanks with the words you think will make sense.

Banana Split

Have you ever made a banana split? It is easy to do. First

you _____ a big bowl. Peel a banana

and _____ it in half from one end

to _____ other. The cut banana goes in

the _____ of the bowl. Next, put three

scoops _____ ice cream on top of the

banana. _____ each scoop of ice cream

with your _____ topping. I like strawberry, hot fudge,

and _____ on mine! When you have the

toppings _____ it is time to cover the whole

_____ with whipped cream. If you like nuts

_____ can sprinkle some chopped peanuts or

almonds _____ the whipped cream. Add a cherry to the

top and you are done! Just one more thing... don't forget to eat it all!

**bottom   Cover   cut   favorite   marshmallow   need
of   on   over   the   thing   you**

Cloze

Cloze is a reading exercise where some of the words are missing and you must put them back in. Read the story below. Every eighth word has been taken out. Fill in the blanks with the words below the story.

Randy The Painter

Randy loved to paint. He liked to paint with his fingers

_____ he was little. He would paint

on _____ . He would paint on tables.

Once he _____ painted on the living room

wall! Randy's _____ were not happy with

his painting. They _____ him to play ball or

ride his _____ . But Randy only wanted to paint.

When _____ was older he helped the neighbors

paint _____ house. He painted a huge but

beautiful _____ on the front of their house.

The _____ did not want a huge beautiful flower

_____ on the front of their house.

Randy _____ that job! Today Randy is very

happy. _____ is a famous painter. Now

his parents _____ his painting. Now the

neighbors wish they had the flower on the front of their house!

begged   bicycle   even   flower   He   lost   love   neighbors
painted   paper   parents   Randy   their   when

Cloze

Cloze is a reading exercise where some of the words are missing and you must put them back in. Read the story below. Every fifth word has been taken out. Fill in the blanks with the words below the story.

Nathan and the Cowboys

Nathan sat as still as he could on the shaky tree branch. No telling

what might _____ if those cowboys

saw _____ . Three cowboys

stood _____ the branch where

Nathan _____ . If they looked

up _____ now they would

see _____ . Nathan held his

breath. _____ cowboys talked and

laughed _____ a few minutes.

They _____ from the tree but

_____ at the edge of

_____ creek. The three

braves _____ to splash each other

_____ play in the water.

_____ relaxed a little.

He _____ forward so he could

_____ them through all the

_____. Suddenly Nathan

lost his _____ and fell. He hit

_____ ground, rolling toward the

_____. He looked up into the faces

of the surprised cowboys!

**and   balance   began   below   creek   for   happen   him   him   leaned
moved   Nathan   right   sat   see   stopped   The   the   the   leaves**

Point of View

A story can be told from three points of view:
- **First person:** The main character tells the story using pronouns such as I, me, we, or us.
- **Limited third person:** A narrator tells the story as if he is watching it happen. Pronouns like he, she, it, they, and them are used.
- **Omniscient third person:** The narrator tells the story as if he is everywhere and knows everything, even what the characters are thinking and feeling.

Read each story and circle the point of view.

Charles stood on the sidewalk. He looked down the street. There was not a person in sight. He bent down and picked up the twenty dollar bill. He folded the bill carefully and put it in his pocket.

First Person   Limited Third Person   Omniscient Third Person

Charles stood on the sidewalk. His stomach was full of butterflies. Should he take the twenty dollar bill that was near his foot? No one was in sight. Charles knew someone would miss that money, but he really needed it. He bent down and picked up the bill. "I won't tell anyone I found it," he thought as he stuffed the money in his pocket.

First Person   Limited Third Person   Omniscient Third Person

I was standing on the sidewalk, thinking about what I could buy with that money. I looked, but did not see a single person on the street. I really needed that twenty dollars! No one needed to know that I found it. I felt uneasy taking the bill, but I quickly stuffed it into my pocket anyway.

First Person   Limited Third Person   Omniscient Third Person

Point of View

A story can be told from three points of view:
-First person: The main character tells the story using pronouns such as I, me, we, or us.
-Limited third person: A narrator tells the story as if he is watching it happen. Pronouns like he, she, it, they, and them are used.
-Omniscient third person: The narrator tells the story as if he is everywhere and knows everything, even what the characters are thinking and feeling.

Read each story and circle the point of view.

I rode my bike up the steep hill. I was so hot and tired. It had been a long race, but I was in the lead! I raced down the other side of the hill. It began to rain a little. The cool wetness felt good on my face.

First Person   Limited Third Person   Omniscient Third Person

It was a hot day. The racers had gotten off to a good start. Susan quickly went ahead of the others. Her face was red and she began to sweat as she rode up the steep hill. It started to rain as she raced down the other side.

First Person   Limited Third Person   Omniscient Third Person

It was a hot day. The racers had gotten off to a good start. Susan quickly pulled ahead of the others. She was excited as she rode up the steep hill. Susan knew she was in the lead. She was hot and tired, but she barely cared. It began to rain as she raced down the other side of the hill. Susan felt cooler as the raindrops splashed her face.

First Person   Limited Third Person   Omniscient Third Person

Point of View

Read each story and circle the point of view.

Buffy the squirrel sat on the fence. He eyed the blue jay carefully. Buffy wondered if he could get that big walnut away from such a big bird. The blue jay rolled the nut across the driveway, pecking at the hard shell. The bird really wanted that nut. Buffy licked his lips and thought about how good that nut was going to taste. He twitched his tail as he tried to decide what to do.

First Person   Limited Third Person   Omniscient Third Person

Buffy the squirrel sat on the fence. He was watching a blue jay on the driveway. The bird had a walnut and was trying to crack it open. The nut rolled across the cement. Buffy's tail twitched as if he was excited. He looked at the nut with eager eyes. He looked as if he was ready to pounce any second.

First Person   Limited Third Person   Omniscient Third Person

I watched that blue jay roll the walnut across the driveway. I could almost taste the nut in my mouth. Oh, would it make a tasty snack! The bird was pecking at the nut, trying to get it open. I wondered how I might steal that tasty tidbit without getting myself pecked by that sharp beak. I twitched my tail to help me think of a good plan. I really wanted that walnut!

First Person   Limited Third Person   Omniscient Third Person

Point of View

A story can be told from three points of view:

-First person: The main character tells the story using pronouns such as I, me, we, or us.

-Limited third person: A narrator tells the story as if he is watching it happen. Pronouns like he, she, it, they, and them are used.

-Omniscient third person: The narrator tells the story as if he is everywhere and knows everything, even what the characters are thinking and feeling.

Read each story and circle the point of view.

Mark raced home as fast as he could. He dumped his books on the kitchen table and opened his notebook. He was barely seated before he began to work on his math problems. The teacher had given the class a huge amount of homework and Mark had the big game this afternoon. He had to finish his school work before he could go out to play. Mark glanced at the clock that was ticking loudly across the room. Only one hour to go. Could he finish in time?

First Person   Limited Third Person   Omniscient Third Person

I ran as fast as I could all the way home. Why did the teacher have to give us so much math homework tonight? I knew Mom would not let me go to the game if I didn't finish my school work first. The guys were counting on me to be at the game. I dumped my books on the kitchen table and got right to work. The ticking clock reminded me that I only had one hour to finish. Could I do it all in time?

First Person   Limited Third Person   Omniscient Third Person

Mark was anxious as he raced home. The teacher had given the class a huge math assignment for tomorrow. This afternoon was the most important ball game of the season. Mark knew his Mom would not let him go to the game if his work was not finished. Mark dumped his books on the kitchen table and got busy right away. He heard the loud ticking of the clock. He looked up and saw that he only had one hour to finish. He felt tense as he rushed through the problems, not caring if they were right or wrong. All Mark wanted to do was finish in time to go to the game. Could he do it?

First Person   Limited Third Person   Omniscient Third Person

Point of View

Read each story and circle the point of view.

Penny and I had come to the library to work on our reports. I found several books and sat down to read them. Penny was looking for information she needed. Suddenly I felt a tapping on my shoulder. Penny put her finger to her lips and motioned for me to follow her. I knew right away that something was wrong. Her face looked white and she was scared. She pulled me behind a stack of books. "I saw that man come in here," she whispered. "The one we saw taking mail from Mrs. Smith's mailbox! Do you think he followed us?" We peeked around the bookshelf and, sure enough, there he was with his back to us.

First Person   Limited Third Person   Omniscient Third Person

Penny and Joan went to the library to work on their reports. Joan found several books and sat down to work. Penny was still looking for books when she saw a man come into the library. Her face turned white and her knees began to shake. Penny quietly tapped Joan's shoulder and motioned to her. The girls slipped behind a stack of books. Penny whispered, "I saw that man come in here. The one we saw taking mail from Mrs. Smith's mailbox! Do you think he followed us?" The girls peeked around the bookshelf and saw the man standing with his back to them.

First Person   Limited Third Person   Omniscient Third Person

Penny and Joan went to the library to work on their reports. Joan found several books and sat down to work. Penny was still looking for her books when she saw a man come into the library. Penny's heart skipped a beat as she recognized him. She knew she had to get to Joan before the man saw them. Penny tapped Joan's shoulder and pulled her behind a stack of books. She whispered, "I saw that man come in here. The one we saw taking mail from Mrs. Smith's mailbox! Do you think he followed us?" Joan felt weak in the knees when she saw the man standing with his back to them.

First Person   Limited Third person   Omniscient Third Person

Compare and Contrast

Compare the words in each row below. Circle the two words that go together then write a sentence telling how they are alike.

1. marsh lagoon plant

_____

_____

2. shimmer dull glow

_____

_____

3. lawyer clerk bride

_____

_____

4. foggy temperature sunny

_____

_____

5. pioneer reindeer hamster

_____

_____

6. vast tiny enormous

_____

_____

7. Halloween Christmas Europe

_____

_____

Think Ahead: Can you find a group that fits all three words in each row ?

Compare and Contrast

Compare the words in each row below. Circle the two words that go together then write a sentence telling how they are alike.

1. karate soccer ball

_____

_____

2. roost nest shed

_____

_____

3. piano radio tuba

_____

_____

4. huge thousand million

_____

_____

5. scare eerie happy

_____

_____

6. baseball hitter batter

_____

_____

7. beetle beast gnat

_____

_____

Think Ahead: Can you find a group that fits all three words in each row ?

Compare and Contrast

Compare the words in each row below. Circle the two words that go together then write a sentence telling how they are alike.

1. harsh   mellow   stern

_____

_____

2. bed   stool   chair

_____

_____

3. stroll   walk   race

_____

_____

4. savage   tame   wild

_____

_____

5. tune   melody   piano

_____

_____

6. tree   limb   branch

_____

_____

7. active   resting   busy

_____

_____

8. grim   funny   serious

_____

_____

Think Ahead: Can you find a group that fits all three words in each row ?

71   CD-3711

Compare and Contrast

Compare the words in each row below. Circle the two words that go together then write a sentence telling how they are alike.

1. grey tan stripe

_____

_____

2. canoe steamship railroad

_____

_____

3. dollar nickel dime

_____

_____

4. hornet wasp butterfly

_____

_____

5. hurricane breeze earthquake

_____

_____

6. icicle frozen sled

_____

_____

Think Ahead: Can you find a group that fits all three words in each row ?

Compare and Contrast

Compare the words in each row below. Circle the two words that go together then write a sentence telling how they are alike.

1. macaroni spaghetti soup

_____

_____

2. fish lobster crab

_____

_____

3. blossom flower leaf

_____

_____

4. sink kitchen oven

_____

_____

5. stone boulder dirt

_____

_____

6. beneath northwest south

_____

_____

7. praise flatter insult

_____

_____

8. midnight month noon

_____

_____

Think Ahead: Can you find a group that fits all three words in each row ?

Prefix "un"

The prefix **un** means "not". Make prefixes out of these words by adding **un** before each word. Use the new words in the sentences below.

lucky   _____

roll   _____

able   _____

certain   _____

kind   _____

cover   _____

easy   _____

friendly   _____

1. Ken was _____ about which path to take back to camp.

2. I was so _____ I couldn't even win at simple games.

3. Kevin was _____ to Sue when he laughed at her mistake.

4. Jack was so _____ he wouldn't even talk to us.

5. Please _____ that box so I can put these blocks in it.

6. The wrapping paper will _____ easily if you pull it just right.

7. Susan felt _____ when the teacher looked at her math test.

8. Kelly is _____ to play outside right now.

Prefix: "un"

The prefix **un** means "not". Make prefixes out of these words by adding **un** before each word. Use the new words in the sentences below.

made   _____

grateful   _____

equal   _____

happy   _____

lit   _____

helpful   _____

hook   _____

necessary   _____

1. The class was _____ when the teacher gave them extra homework.

2. A history book is _____ when I am looking for answers to science questions.

3. It was _____ to drive all the way to the bank because I had money in my pocket.

4. The spoiled child was _____ for all his new gifts.

5. An _____ room is very dark at midnight.

6. Can you _____ those drapes for me, please?

7. Our pieces of cake are _____. Yours is larger than mine!

8. We left the beds _____ this morning because we were in a hurry.

Prefix: "Re"

The prefix **re** means "again". Make prefixes out of these words by adding **re** before each word. Use the new words in the sentences below.

do   _____

call   _____

write   _____

mark   _____

paint   _____

live   _____

move   _____

name   _____

1. Joey must _____ his math problems because they are all wrong.

2. Mary will use soap and water to _____ the stain from her blouse.

3. I thought I heard you make a _____ about my new boots.
   Did you say you liked them?

4. The old paint is peeling off the house. We will have to _____
   it soon.

5. I have to _____ this paper because there are too many words
   spelled wrong.

6. Can you _____ what you did on your last birthday?

7. We will _____ our clubhouse because we don't like the
   name "Tigers" anymore.

8. I do not like to _____ memories that are painful to me.

Prefix: "Re"

The prefix **re** means "again". Make prefixes out of these words by adding **re** before each word. Use the new words in the sentences below.

mind _____

place _____

wind _____

word _____

make _____

turn _____

wash _____

heat _____

1. You will have to _____ the bed because you did not do a good job the first time.

2. Mom said we have to _____ this video tape before we can play another one.

3. Do not break this glass because it is very old and I cannot _____ it.

4. I do not like the way my paper sounds. Can you help me _____ it?

5. The wind blew the clean sheets off the clothesline. Now we have to _____ all of them.

6. Please _____ my soup because it has become cold.

7. It is time to _____ these library books!

8. Can you _____ me that I have to leave at four o'clock? I tend to forget sometimes.

Prefix: "Under"

The prefix **under** means "below". Make prefixes out of these words by adding **under** before each word. Use the new words in the sentences below.

foot   _____

cover   _____

water   _____

ground   _____

wear   _____

done   _____

ripe   _____

weight   _____

1. The doctor said Jimmy is a little _____ . He needs to put on ten pounds by next month.

2. It rained so hard our street was _____ and we couldn't go anywhere.

3. That pineapple is _____ and not ready to eat yet.

4. The policeman had to go _____ to catch the thief.

5. A subway is a train that travels _____.

6. Our new puppy was _____, causing us to trip all the time.

7. My aunt always gives me new _____ for my birthday.

8. The meat was _____ and we had to cook it more before we could eat it.

Prefix: "After"

The prefix **after** means "after or later". Make prefixes out of these words by adding **after** before each word. Use the new words in the sentences below.

noon   _____

taste   _____

thought   _____

llfe   _____

ward   _____

care   _____

glow   _____

time   _____

1. The school has _____ so children can stay until dinner time.

2. The flash from the camera had an _____, lighting the room for a few seconds.

3. We are going on a picnic this _____.

4. The onions left a strong _____ in my mouth.

5. Many people believe that there is an _____ when we die.

6. Steve had an _____ when he had finished speaking. He wrote it down so he wouldn't forget it.

7. We will go to the movie now and get a hamburger _____.

8. The _____ is the future!

Prefix: "Mis"

The prefix **mis** means "bad". Make prefixes out of these words by adding **mis** before each word. Use the new words in the sentences below.

behaving   _____

fortune   _____

take   _____

lead   _____

laid   _____

adventure   _____

matched   _____

read   _____

1. I am afraid I have _____ the keys again. I cannot find them anywhere.

2. After our last _____ , I am afraid to try skiing again.

3. David made only one _____ on his spelling test!

4. The children were _____ and were sent to the principal's office.

5. Yesterday I had the _____ of breaking my leg.

6. Kevin had on a _____ pair of socks. One was black and the other was brown!

7. Sally _____ the sign. She thought it said "field" instead of "yield".

8. I did not mean to _____ you about the play. I said you had a part in it, but I did not say you were the star!

               CD-3711

Prefix: "Out"

The prefix **out** means "beyond". Make prefixes out of these words by adding **out** before each word. Use the new words in the sentences below.

last   _____

run   _____

do   _____

live   _____

number   _____

rage   _____

look   _____

grow   _____

1. Daniel is getting such big feet he will soon _____ those shoes!

2. Tina always has a happy _____ on life. She thinks everything that happens is good.

3. Our cat is much younger than our dog. The cat will probably _____ the dog by a few years.

4. I cannot _____ your science project because it is the best one I have ever seen!

5. There are seven boys and only three girls at the party. The boys _____ the girls.

6. I am drinking my soda slowly. My drink will _____ yours because you are gulping your soda quickly.

7. I'll bet I can _____ you in a foot race!

8. Beth flew into a _____ when she learned she did not win the contest.

Prefix: "Over"

The prefix **over** means "too much". Make prefixes out of these words by adding **over** before each word. Use the new words in the sentences below.

heat   _____

stuffed   _____

price   _____

looks   _____

board   _____

acts   _____

dressed   _____

fill   _____

1. Bill never gets a part in the play because he _____ at tryouts.

2. My uncle fell _____ when we went sailing last week.

3. Do not _____ your cookies or no one will want to buy them.

4. Do not _____ the gas tank or it will spill on the ground.

5. Kathy wore a velvet dress to the pool party. She was very _____ .

6. Our bedroom window _____ a beautiful park below.

7. If you _____ the soup it will burn your mouth!

8. I ate too much dinner and now I am _____ !

Prefix: "Be"

The prefix **be** means "make". Make prefixes out of these words by adding **be** before each word. Use the new words in the sentences below.

side   _____

friend   _____

cause   _____

come   _____

witch   _____

hind   _____

ware   _____

low   _____

1. Vicky put the forks _____ the plates as she set the table.

2. Hang your hat on the hook just _____ mine.

3. It is important to _____ when you are walking alone at night.

4. Watch out! It is said that a cat can _____ you on Halloween night.

5. I will _____ a better speller when I learn to check my work.

6. Connie would like to _____ the new girl because she seems
    so lonely.

7. Do not stand _____ the door or you may get hit when someone
    opens it.

8. John must go to bed early tonight _____ he is going fishing early
    tomorrow morning.

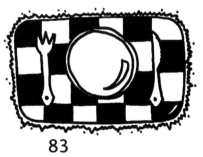

Contractions

Read the sentences below. Circle the correct contraction for the underlined words.

1. I am going to the zoo tomorrow.
   I'd   I'll   I'm

2. You are my best friend!
   you'd   you'll   you're

3. Are you sure we are on the right path?
   we'd   we'll   we're

4. Brian said he is older than you.
   he'd   he's   he'll

5. I think these will make fine curtains for the clubhouse.
   there's   these'll   they'll

6. I did not look at the movie when it was scary!
   didn't   did'nt   don't

7. Who would want to live in that dusty old house?
   who'd   who's   who've

8. We might not need to cut the grass this week.
   might've   mightn't   mayn't

9. I do not have the right book, but this will do just fine.
   it'll   that'll   this'll

10. They are very kind people.
    They'll   They're   They've

Contractions

Read the sentences below. Circle the correct contraction for the underlined words.

1. Lucy <u>does not</u> like to swim in the lake.
   don't   didn't   doesn't

2. Mother said that <u>she would</u> take us to the park today.
   she'll   she'd   she's

3. <u>Who are</u> those new people that just moved here?
   Who'll   Who're   Who's

4. We <u>have not</u> had time to unpack our suitcases yet.
   hadn't   hasn't   haven't

5. Do you think we <u>could have</u> missed the right turn?
   can't   couldn't   could've

6. Do you think <u>you will</u> want a snack before bedtime?
   you'll   you're   you've

7. We <u>are not</u> really sure who the sweater belongs to.
   are'nt   aren't   isn't

8. Mrs. Jones was certain that <u>there would</u> be enough food for all our guests.
   there'll   there'd   there's

9. <u>Who is</u> going to the lake with us?
   Who'll   Who's   Won't

10. Judy said that <u>they will</u> be a little late getting here.
    they'd   they'll   they've

Contractions

Read the sentences below. Circle the correct contraction for the underlined words.

1. <u>Let us</u> move on to the next room of the museum now.
    Lets   Let's   Let'us

2. We <u>should have</u> known that Carol would be late. She always is!
    shouldn't   should't   should've

3. The books <u>were not</u> on the shelves where they belonged.
    wasn't   weren't   where'd

4. <u>You have</u> to do your homework before you can go out to play.
    You'll   You're   You've

5. Patty promised <u>that will</u> be the best cake she has ever baked.
    that'd   that'll   that's

6. Amy said <u>she would</u> love to go to the show with Mike.
    she'd   she'll   she's

7. <u>That is</u> my favorite pair of pants.
    That'd   That'll   That's

8. I told you I <u>would not</u> have any candy left by the end of the day!
    won't   wouldn't   would've

9. <u>I have</u> at least six more pages to write before I will be done.
    I'd   I'm   I've

10. I <u>will not</u> use any of your paper if you would rather I did not.
    wasn't   willn't   won't

Name _____

Contractions

Read the sentences below. Circle the correct contraction for the underlined words.

1. <u>What will</u> you bring to the party?
   What'd   What'll   What's

2. Mark and Tracy said <u>they have</u> been waiting for over an hour to get tickets.
   they'll   they're   they've

3. <u>Those will</u> be the biggest pancakes we have ever made!
   That'll   Those'll   These'll

4. <u>Who will</u> go shopping with me?
   Who'd   Who'll   Who's

5. John said <u>he will</u> be happy to fix the car for us.
   he'll   he'd   he's

6. <u>They are</u> a great group of children!
   They'd   They're   They'll

7. I <u>could not</u> see over the fence so I looked through the gate.
   can't   could'nt   couldn't

8. Billy enjoys eating donuts. He thinks <u>they are</u> very sweet tasting.
   they'll   they're   they've

9. Karen knows she <u>should not</u> be angry with her sister.
   shouldn't   should've   can't

10. Nancy <u>had not</u> noticed the sign for the wet paint.
   hadn't   had'nt   hasn't

Contractions

Read the sentences below. Circle the correct contraction for the underlined words.

1. <u>What would</u> you think if you saw a pink elephant?
      What's   What'd   What'll

2. Martha thinks <u>she is</u> the smartest girl in school.
      she'd   she'll   she's

3. <u>We will</u> be the first ones at the party if we leave now.
      We'd   We'll   We're

4. <u>There have</u> been six flights into space this past month.
      There'd   They've   There've

5. I can see that <u>it is</u> getting pretty late.
      it's   it'll   I've

6. The door <u>was not</u> locked all night.
      wasn't   won't   wouldn't

7. You <u>need not</u> have bothered getting the guest room ready because we are not staying.
      needn't   didn't   should've

8. <u>Who will</u> go first?
      Who'll   Who're   Who's

9. Bobby said he <u>can not</u> come to my house after school today.
      can't   couldn't   could've

10. <u>There will</u> be a short rest time after we finish walking this mile.
      There'll   There's   There've

Suffixes

Words are changed when you add a suffix to them. Put the right word in each sentence.

excite excitement

1. Watching a good movie can _____ me. The _____ makes me happy.

add addition

2. The new room is an _____ to our house.   We had to _____ the room because we needed more space.

sell seller

3. Joe likes to _____ cars. He is a _____ for the Used Car Company.

active activity

4. Mrs. Kline likes to stay _____ and do many things. She says the _____ makes her feel healthy.

light lighten

5. Dad put a new _____ in my bedroom. He said the room was a little dark and we needed to _____ it.

spoon spoonful

6. I need a _____ to mix the cookie dough. Please add a _____ of water because it is too dry.

depart departing

7. The airplane will be _____ in one hour. It is time for us to _____ for the airport.

brave bravery

8. Roger is a very _____ boy. He even got a medal for his _____ .

Name _____   skill: suffixes

Suffixes

Words are changed when you add a suffix to them. Put the right word in
each sentence.

amuse amusement

1. Bob loves to _____ his friends by acting like a clown.
His friends like the _____ of watching him.

wisp wispy

2. Lauren pushed a _____ of hair out of her face. She
needed a haircut because her hair was too _____ around
her face.

speak speaker

3. I was asked to be the main _____ to make the
presentation for my club. I will have to _____ in front of a
lot of people!

respect respectful

4. My mother says I must be _____ of older people. It is
important to show my _____ .

explore exploration

5. Jim loves to _____ caves. He thinks that cave
_____ is more fun than anything.

pain painful

6. I have a _____ sore on the bottom of my foot. Every
step I take causes me more _____ .

tingle tingled

7. Her fingers _____ as she felt the electricity run
through them. Even the top of her arms began to _____

value valuable

8. This old coin is very _____ . I don't know the exact
_____ , but I do know it is worth a lot of money.

Suffixes

Words are changed when you add a suffix to them. Put the right word in each sentence.

decorate decorations

1. It is fun to _____ the classroom for a holiday. My favorite _____ are the balloons that float to the ceiling.

perform performance

2. Erin will _____ on stage next week. She is practicing so her _____ will be the best she can do.

thrill thrilling

3. I find it _____ to sit in the front row at the movies. When the movie gets scary it is a real _____ to me!

fear fearless

4. My brother has no _____ of dark rooms. He is _____ and can walk right in without turning on the light.

begin beginner

5. I will _____ to take piano lessons next week. I am in the _____ class.

select selection

6. Kim must _____ a gift for her best friend. She will make her _____ at the gift shop in town.

easy easily

7. Simon _____ won the spelling contest. Spelling is a subject that is very _____ for him.

argue argument

8. I _____ a lot with my brother. Just this morning we had an _____ over whose turn it was to clean our room.

Suffixes

Words are changed when you add a suffix to them. Put the right word in
each sentence.

create creation

1. Jan loves to _____ animals with her clay. Her latest
_____ was a creature with three legs and four eyes.

stitch stitching

2. Mother was _____ my old play clothes when I came
rushing in the room. She took the last _____ before she
asked me what I wanted.

exhibit exhibited

3. Tony was going to _____ his black rabbit at the fair
this year. Last year Tony took first place when he _____
his white rabbit.

garden gardener

4. Mr. Potts is a great _____ . His
_____ is the best one in town.

invent inventor

5. I believe I will _____ something important one day.
My dream is to be a famous _____ .

advertise advertisement

6. The bakery always has an _____ in the window.
They like to _____ because it makes people come in
to shop there.

lazy lazily

7. Today feels like a _____ day. I stayed in bed and
_____ watched as the sun climbed high in the sky.

Suffixes

Words are changed when you add a suffix to them. Put the right word in each sentence.

number numerous

1. Jill has _____ pencils in her pencil box. There are so many I can't count to the _____ she has!

relation relationship

2. My mother is my favorite _____ . We have a very close _____ .

astonish astonishment

3. I watched in _____ as the magician did the trick with fire. It takes a lot to _____ me, but he was really good!

congratulate congratulations

4. The judge said _____ to Jimmy, the winner of the science fair. I went over to _____ him, too.

suggest suggestions

5. There was a box for _____ by the door. I knew what I wanted to _____ so I wrote it down and put it in the box.

believe believable

6. I don't think this story is very _____ . I do not _____ in monsters or witches anymore.

warn warning

7. Alice tried to _____ the boaters that a storm was quickly moving in. Her _____ came too late. The boaters were caught in the raging storm.

neat neatly

8. Sharon hung her clothes _____ on their hangers. She liked to keep her room _____ and tidy.

Multiple Meanings

Many words have more than one meaning. Sometimes you can figure out which meaning is correct by seeing how the word was used in a sentence. If you cannot figure it out, look the word up in the dictionary.

In each sentence below a word has been underlined. There are two definitions given for the underlined word. Decide which meaning is correct by reading the sentence and thinking about how the word was used. Write the correct meaning on the line.

1. The <u>bail</u> was broken so the bucket full of water was difficult to lift.
    a. throw water out   b.handle of a pail

    _____

2. The princess had a grand time at the <u>ball</u> last night.
    a. a dance   b. a round object

    _____

3. The rabbit <u>hide</u> will make a warm pair of mittens.
    a. to keep out of sight   b. an animal skin

    _____

4. Joe <u>left</u> before I could tell him goodbye.
    a. the opposite of right   b. went away

    _____

5. Jack had a <u>fit</u> when his brother broke his new bicycle.
    a. suitable   b. sudden attack

    _____

6. The group became <u>grave</u> when they saw the danger they were in.
    a. serious   b. a place of burial

    _____

7. The <u>mortar</u> between the bricks was beginning to crumble.
    a. a cement mixture   b. a short cannon

    _____

8. The crash was so hard it <u>jarred</u> my body!
    a. a container   b. rattled

    _____

Multiple Meanings

Many words have more than one meaning. Sometimes you can figure out which meaning is correct by seeing how the word was used in a sentence. If you cannot figure it out, look the word up in the dictionary.

In each sentence below a word has been underlined. There are two definitions given for the underlined word. Decide which meaning is correct by reading the sentence and thinking about how the word was used. Write the correct meaning on the line.

1. The boy was <u>lean</u> because he ate healthy foods and exercised.
   a. slanting   b. not fat

   _____

2. The farmer built a new <u>pen</u> to keep the pigs in.
   a. writing tool   b. enclosed yard

   _____

3. Kathy was dizzy so she held on to the chair to <u>stable</u> herself.
   a. building for horses   b. steady

   _____

4. That Nancy can sure <u>yak!</u> She kept me on the phone for two hours!
   a. talk endlessly   b. a long-haired ox

   _____

5. Go to the kitchen <u>tap</u> and fill this bottle with water.
   a. strike lightly   b. faucet

   _____

6. This table is built so well, it should <u>last</u> forever.
   a. at the end   b. continue

   _____

7. Sam needs a smaller <u>bit</u> for this hole. The one he has is too big for the screw.
   a. did bite   b. tool for drilling

   _____

8. The puppy will <u>cock</u> his head when he is puzzled.
   a. tilt upward   b. rooster

   _____

Multiple Meanings

Many words have more than one meaning. Sometimes you can figure out which meaning is correct by seeing how the word was used in a sentence. If you cannot figure it out, look the word up in the dictionary.

In each sentence below a word has been underlined. There are two definitions given for the underlined word. Decide which meaning is correct by reading the sentence and thinking about how the word was used. Write the correct meaning on the line.

1. I do not mean to <u>carp</u>, but I am tired of telling you to clean your room.
    a. complain   b. kind of fish

    _____

2. Justin wants to <u>mine</u> for diamonds on his land.
    a. belonging to me   b. hole in the earth

    _____

3. Please draw a <u>ring</u> around the correct answer.
    a. circle   b. bell sound

    _____

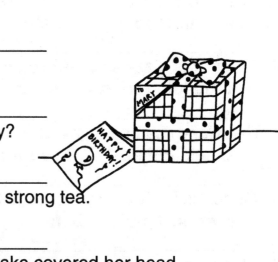

4. Do you have a <u>present</u> for Mary's birthday party?
    a. not absent   b. gift

    _____

5. <u>Steep</u> the tea bag for three minutes if you want strong tea.
    a. having a sharp slope   b. soak

    _____

6. The swimmer was almost drowned when the <u>wake</u> covered her head.
    a. stop sleeping   b. trail left behind a ship

    _____

7. This was a job <u>well</u> done!
    a. satisfactory   b. hole dug for water

    _____

8. The nurse will <u>tend</u> to your cut now.
    a. take care of   b. incline to

    _____

Name _____

Multiple Meanings

Many words have more than one meaning. Sometimes you can figure out which meaning is correct by seeing how the word was used in a sentence. If you cannot figure it out, look the word up in the dictionary.

In each sentence below a word has been underlined. There are two definitions given for the underlined word. Decide which meaning is correct by reading the sentence and thinking about how the word was used. Write the correct meaning on the line.

1. Did you see Jim <u>vault</u> that fence without even touching it?
   a. a safe for valuables   b. jump over

   _____

2. Put the string on this <u>reel</u> so we can use it next time.
   a. spool for winding   b. lively dance

   _____

3. Abbey and I played three games of <u>pool</u> this weekend.
   a. tank with water   b. a game with balls on a table

   _____

4. The angry driver began to <u>rail</u> at the bus driver who ran into his car.
   a. bar of wood or metal   b. complain bitterly

   _____

5. This movie is very much <u>like</u> the book I just read.
   a. similar to   b. be pleased with

   _____

6. John is the <u>elder</u> of the two boys.
   a. older   b. small tree

   _____

7. The chef poured the <u>batter</u> into a large baking pan.
   a. liquid   b. baseball player

   _____

8. We can <u>alight</u> from the airplane now.
   a. get down from   b. on fire

   _____

Multiple Meanings

Many words have more than one meaning. Sometimes you can figure out which meaning is correct by seeing how the word was used in a sentence. If you cannot figure it out, look the word up in the dictionary.

In each sentence below a word has been underlined. There are two definitions given for the underlined word. Decide which meaning is correct by reading the sentence and thinking about how the word was used. Write the correct meaning on the line.

1. The boys blazed a path through the thick underbrush.
   a. fire   b. marked a trail

   _____

2. Dad cooked the chop a little too much and it tasted dry.
   a. cut with something sharp   b. cut of meat

   _____

3. Clip on the papers so they stay together.
   a. cut   b. fasten

   _____

4. The present was in a large box wrapped in brown paper.
   a. four sided container   b. to fight with fists

   _____

5. My jeans are beginning to fray a little at the bottom.
   a. become ragged   b. fight

   _____

6. The sailor closed the hatch so the water could not get in his room.
   a. come out of an egg   b. an opening in the deck

   _____

7. The nap of the carpet is wearing down.
   a. short sleep   b. rug fuzz

   _____

8. The mole dug tunnels all over our front lawn.
   a. brown spot on the skin   b. small underground animal

   _____

Name _____   skill: multiple meanings

Multiple Meanings

Many words have more than one meaning. Sometimes you can figure out which meaning is correct by seeing how the word was used in a sentence. If you cannot figure it out, look the word up in the dictionary.

In each sentence below a word has been underlined. There are two definitions given for the underlined word. Decide which meaning is correct by reading the sentence and thinking about how the word was used. Write the correct meaning on the line.

1. Joel burned his palm on the hot stove.
   a. inside of the hand   b. kind of tree

   _____

2. Kelly cut a spray from the rose bush.
   a. sprinkle liquid   b. small branch with leaves and flowers

   _____

3. I found a slug in the garden.
   a. small slow-moving animal   b. to hit hard

   _____

4. The toll on the bridge was one dollar.
   a. sound of a bell   b. fee paid to use something

   _____

5. Grandma liked to sit on the front stoop and watch the neighborhood.
   a. bend down   b. porch

   _____

6. Greg will take six of the pencils and you can have the rest.
   a. sleep   b. what is left

   _____

7. Please get the clippers and prune that bush.
   a. fruit   b. trim

   _____

8. Mrs. Smith has six boys to rear.
   a. the back part   b. bring up

   _____

©1995 Kelley Wingate Publications, Inc.   99   CD-3711

Multiple Meanings

Many words have more than one meaning. Sometimes you can figure out which meaning is correct by seeing how the word was used in a sentence. If you cannot figure it out, look the word up in the dictionary.

In each sentence below a word has been underlined. There are two definitions given for the underlined word. Decide which meaning is correct by reading the sentence and thinking about how the word was used. Write the correct meaning on the line.

1. The <u>husky</u> was strong enough to pull the sled by himself!
    a. big and strong   b. a kind of dog

    _____

2. Karen was so weak her legs and arms were <u>limp</u>.
    a. lame walk   b. not stiff

    _____

3. Jane wore a <u>jumper</u> to school today.
    a. person or thing that jumps   b. type of dress

    _____

4. If I can get their map I might be able to <u>foil</u> their plans for the robbery.
    a. prevent or stop   b. metal wrapping

    _____

5. The balloon was <u>grazing</u> the ceiling.
    a. feed on grass   b. gently touching

    _____

6. It is not healthy to <u>fast</u> for more than a day or two.
    a. go without food   b. speedy

    _____

7. A <u>crow</u> made a nest in the old pine tree.
    a. loud cry of a rooster   b. large black bird

    _____

8. Poor Donna has a <u>case</u> of the measles!
    a. condition   b. box or container

    _____

Multiple Meanings

Many words have more than one meaning. Sometimes you can figure out which meaning is correct by seeing how the word was used in a sentence. If you cannot figure it out, look the word up in the dictionary.

In each sentence below a word has been underlined. There are two definitions given for the underlined word. Decide which meaning is correct by reading the sentence and thinking about how the word was used. Write the correct meaning on the line.

1. I do not like long speeches because they <u>bore</u> me.
    a. make a hole   b. make weary

    _____

2. Sammy can <u>bowl</u> very well at Park Ten Lanes.
    a. rounded dish   b. play a game with pins and a ball

    _____

3. The cold winter weather can <u>chap</u> your hands quickly.
    a. crack or roughen   b. boy or man

    _____

4. The woman did not <u>bat</u> an eyelash at the high price she was charged.
    a. flying mammal   b. wink

    _____

5. We put a <u>band</u> around the cards to keep them together.
    a. group of musicians   b. thin strip that binds

    _____

6. The <u>bank</u> was slippery and muddy so we walked in the water.
    a. a place of business   b. land along a river

    _____

7. The man had a <u>bass</u> voice that sounded warm and nice.
    a. low sound   b. kind of fish

    _____

8. The boat began to <u>bob</u> as the waves grew bigger.
    a. nickname for Robert   b. move up and down

    _____

Multiple Meanings

Many words have more than one meaning. Sometimes you can figure out which meaning is correct by seeing how the word was used in a sentence. If you cannot figure it out, look the word up in the dictionary.

In each sentence below a word has been underlined. There are two definitions given for the underlined word. Decide which meaning is correct by reading the sentence and thinking about how the word was used. Write the correct meaning on the line.

1. The coyote will <u>bay</u> at a full moon.
    a. part of a sea   b. howl

    _____

2. The town began to <u>boom</u> as more people moved there.
    a. sudden increase in size   b. deep sound

    _____

3. I am <u>bound</u> to become a movie star some day!
    a. on the way   b. spring back

    _____

4. Who made this delicious blueberry <u>cobbler?</u>
    a. one who mends shoes   b. fruit pie with one crust

    _____

5. Mark took a walk around the <u>compound</u> before turning in for the night.
    a. having more than one part   b. enclosed yard

    _____

6. Take a <u>count</u> to see if everyone is here.
    a. name numbers in order   b. a nobleman

    _____

7. The pies were sitting on the <u>counter</u> in the kitchen.
    a. long table top   b. one who counts

    _____

8. What is the <u>date</u> for the fair this year?
    a. day, month, and year   b. sweet dark fruit

    _____

Multiple Meanings

Many words have more than one meaning. Sometimes you can figure out which meaning is correct by seeing how the word was used in a sentence. If you cannot figure it out, look the word up in the dictionary.

In each sentence below a word has been underlined. There are two definitions given for the underlined word. Decide which meaning is correct by reading the sentence and thinking about how the word was used. Write the correct meaning on the line.

1. My boss said he would <u>dock</u> my pay if I am late once more.
    a. wharf   b. cut some off

    _____

2. The best pillows are made of <u>down</u>.
    a. soft feathers   b. grassy land

    _____

3. I must say that Brad is a sharp <u>dresser</u>.
    a. one who dresses   b. chest of drawers

    _____

4. We rented a <u>flat</u> with two bedrooms.
    a. smooth   b. apartment

    _____

5. The deer was <u>fleet</u> so we didn't see her for long.
    a. group of ships   b. quick

    _____

6. It is time to <u>file</u> some of these papers!
    a. to put in order in a drawer   b. to smooth the rough edges

    _____

7. Meghan tripped over a rock and began to <u>flounder</u> in the shallow water.
    a. struggle   b. kind of fish

    _____

8. <u>Hail</u> a cab so we won't have to walk in the rain.
    a. pieces of ice that fall like rain   b. shout or call out to

    _____

Analogies

Analogies compare relationships of words. For example:

chair is to sit as bed is to _____

The relationship of chair and sit (you sit in a chair) is compared to the relationship between bed and what you do in it (you sleep in a bed). The missing word is sleep.

Find the missing word in these analogies.

in is to out as up is to _____

two is to four as three is to _____

snow is to cold as sun is to _____

mother is to aunt as father is to _____

ear is to hear as eye is to _____

she is to her as he is to _____

dog is to bark as bird is to _____

brother is to boy as sister is to _____

bear is to den as bee is to _____

finger is to hand as toe is to _____

girl is to mother as boy is to _____

left is to right as top is to _____

Analogies 2

Analogies compare relationships of words. For example:
chair is to sit as bed is to _____
The relationship of chair and sit (you sit in a chair) is compared to the relationship between bed and what you do in it (you sleep in a bed). The missing word is sleep.

Find the missing word in these analogies.

car is to driver as plane is to _____

bird is to sky as fish is to _____

coffee is to drink as hamburger is to _____

small is to tiny as large is to _____

glove is to hand as boot is to _____

easy is to simple as hard is to _____

breakfast is to lunch as morning is to _____

blue is to color as round is to _____

date is to calendar as time is to _____

win is to lose as stop is to _____

minute is to hour as day is to _____

paw is to dog as fin is to _____

Analogies 3

Analogies compare relationships of words. For example:
chair is to sit as bed is to _____
The relationship of chair and sit (you sit in a chair) is compared to the relationship between bed and what you do in it (you sleep in a bed). The missing word is sleep.

Find the missing word in these analogies.

moon is to earth as earth is to _____

tree is to lumber as wheat is to _____

library is to books as kitchen is to _____

three is to six as four is to _____

princess is to queen as prince is to _____

story is to read as song is to _____

length is to weight as inches is to _____

blind is to deaf as see is to _____

pen is to write as broom is to _____

wrist is to hand as ankle is to _____

water is to ship as air is to _____

engine is to go as brake is to _____

CD-3711

Analogies 4

Analogies compare relationships of words. For example:
chair is to sit as bed is to _____
The relationship of chair and sit (you sit in a chair) is compared to the relationship between bed and what you do in it (you sleep in a bed). The missing word is sleep.

Find the missing word in these analogies.

glass is to break as paper is to _____

soap is to clean as mud is to _____

silk is to smooth as sandpaper is to _____

penny is to dollar as inch is to _____

in is to out as hot is to _____

frown is to angry as smile is to _____

fat is to thin as dark is to _____

screwdriver is to hammer as screw is to _____

cowboy is to cow as shepherd is to _____

cat is to kitten as dog is to _____

mother is to daughter as father is to _____

lawn is to grass as beach is to _____

Answer Key

Name _____   skill: comprehension

What Are Symbols

Symbols are drawings or letters that stand for something else. Right now you are reading symbols. Letters on this page stand for sounds that we use when speaking. When the letters are put together they are symbols for words that we speak. Symbols are full of meaning. They express, or tell, feelings about something. For example, every school has a symbol of their sports teams. Schools can choose tigers or lions as team symbols. These animals symbolize, or stand for, strength and a fearless team. There are many symbols we use every day. The flag is a symbol of our country. Each television station uses a symbol so we can recognize, or identify who they are, at a glance. Restaurants have symbols. Even bathroom doors have symbols to help us recognize them. Symbols are an important part of our lives.

1. What is the main idea of this story?
   a. Symbols are drawings
   (b.) Symbols help us recognize things
   c. Symbols are an important part of our lives
2. What are symbols?

   Drawings or letters

3. The word "express" means:
   (a.) tell
   b. letter
   c. symbol
4. What word means identify?
   a. symbolize
   (b.) recognize
   c. express
5. Why do schools pick symbols for their sports teams?

   To stand for strength and
   fearlessness
6. What does our flag symbolize?

   Things important to our country

THINK AHEAD: What are three symbols you see every day?

©1995 Kelley Wingate Publications, Inc.   4   KW 1014

Name _____   skill: comprehension

Phoenix

The phoenix bird is one of the oldest symbols that is still used today. Phoenix was the Greek name for a fictional, or make-believe, bird that was important to the sun god in ancient Egypt. The phoenix was a bird that looked like an eagle with red and gold feathers. The story is that the bird lived for 500 years. At the end of its life, the phoenix would build a big fire and burn itself to death. When the fire was gone, a new phoenix would rise from the ashes and begin its 500 years of life. The phoenix can be found in stories, religious ceremonies, and even government symbols. This bird symbolized the rising and setting of the sun. Later in history the phoenix became known as the symbol of death and resurrection, or life after death.

1. What is the main idea of this story?
   (a.) The phoenix bird is an ancient symbol that is still used.
   b. The phoenix is a bird.
   c. There are stories about the phoenix.
2. What does the phoenix look like?

   an eagle with red and gold
   feathers
3. What does "fictional" mean?
   a. sun god
   (b.) not real
   c. eagle
4. How many years does the phoenix live?

   500
5. What happens to the phoenix at the end of its life?

   It burns itself to death
6. What does "resurrection" mean?
   a. make-believe
   b. symbols
   (c.) come to life after you have died

THINK AHEAD: Why might governments use the symbol of the phoenix?

©1995 Kelley Wingate Publications, Inc.   5   KW 1014

Name _____   skill: comprehension

Chrysanthemum

The chrysanthemum is a flower than is commonly called the "mum". It has been popular in Japan for many years. But there is one Japanese city, Himeji, that will not grow the mum. Those people think it is unlucky to even touch the mum. There is a legend in Himeji about a servant girl who lived a long time ago. The girl was named O-Kiku, which means Chrysanthemum Blossom. O-Kiku had the job of taking care of ten golden plates. One day she found that one of the plates was missing. She thought she would be blamed for taking the plate and that would bring dishonor, or shame, to her family. O-Kiku threw herself into a well and drowned. It is said that every night her ghost returns to count the plates. When the ghost gets to nine it screams and begins to count again. People of the city believe that the chrysanthemum is still unlucky, so they do not grow them.

1. What is the main idea of this story?
   a. One golden plate was missing.
   (b.) The chrysanthemum symbolizes bad luck.
   c. The Japanese like chrysanthemums.
2. What are chrysanthemums?

   flowers
3. The name "O-Kiku" means:
   (a.) chrysanthemum blossom
   b. flower
   c. shame
4. What is the name of the city that will not grow mums?

   Himeji
5. What is another word for "shame"?
   a. mum
   b. O-Kiku
   (c.) dishonor
6. What happened to O-Kiku?

   She threw herself into a well
   and drowned

THINK AHEAD: As young children we sometimes think stepping on the cracks in the sidewalk is unlucky. What are some other things that we think are unlucky?

©1995 Kelley Wingate Publications, Inc.   6   KW 1014

Name _____   skill: comprehension

Crowns

Crowns are ornaments worn on the head to symbolize authority, or power. Kings and queens wore crowns. The earliest crowns are from ancient Egypt. Egypt had two kingdoms and each king wore a crown. When the two kingdoms united, or joined together, the crowns were also put together and made into a double crown. The double crown symbolized the joining of the two kingdoms. Ancient Greece had crowns but they were not for kings. Greek crowns were made of leaves and flowers and were worn by winners of sports contests! China had a kind of crown called the diadem. The diadem was a band of silk that was tied around the forehead. This band would often have fancy designs and jewels sewn on it. The tiara is a smaller kind of crown that is often worn by women. The crown given at beauty contests is a tiara. This crown is a metal band that has rows of stones or ornaments in the front. Crowns are symbols that everyone recognizes. They show that the wearer is an important person.

1. What is the main idea of this story?
   a. Kings and queens wear crowns.
   (b.) Crowns are symbols of power.
   c. Tiaras are types of crowns.
2. What do crowns symbolize?

   authority
3. What did the double crown of Egypt mean?

   two kingdoms were joined together
4. The word "authority" means:
   (a.) power
   b. crown
   c. diadem
5. What is a diadem?

   a band of silk tied around the forehead
6. Describe a tiara.

   a metal band with rows of stones or
   ornaments in the front

THINK AHEAD: Why do you think crowns were chosen as the symbol of kings and queens?

©1995 Kelley Wingate Publications, Inc.   7   KW 1014

Answer Key

Name _____ skill: comprehension

Heraldry

Knights wore suits of armor, metal that covered the body. When a knight was fully dressed in his armor it was difficult to tell who he was. Knights began to paint badges or symbols on their armor so they could be recognized easily. Each knight picked a symbol that stood for who he was or what he was like. For example, a man named Oakes might choose an oak tree because it was a picture of his name. Other men chose beasts like the lion or eagle because they were brave and strong. Other symbols were simple bold designs because they were easy to recognize, even from a distance. These badges became known as a coat of arms, the symbol of a family name. People called heralds were experts who could easily identify any coat of arms. The custom of having a coat of arms can still be found in many parts of Europe and Asia and is known as heraldry.

1. **What is the main idea of this story?**
   a. It was hard to tell who each knight was.
   b. Heralds could read every coat of arms.
   c. Heraldry is a symbol for a family name.
2. **Why did knights need a coat of arms?**
   So people could tell who he was.
3. **The word "armor" means:**
   a. coat of arms
   b. a suit of metal
   c. experts
4. **How did a knight choose his coat of arms?**
   He picked a symbol that stood for who he was or what he was like.
5. **What is a coat of arms?**
   a. a symbol of a family name
   b. a coat made out of arms
   c. a trumpet
6. **What job did heralds do?**
   Easily identify coats of arms

THINK AHEAD: Design a coat of arms for your family name.

©1995 Kelley Wingate Publications, Inc.   8   KW 1014

Name _____ skill: comprehension

Eagle

Eagles are large birds that are powerful and brave hunters. Eagles can be found on every continent except Antarctica. They have been symbols of power and courage since ancient, or very old, times. Pictures of eagles can be found on ancient buildings in Egypt. Indians wore eagle feathers to show others that they were very brave. There used to be a lot of eagles, but they are becoming rare. They have been hunted and captured. They have also been killed by chemicals used to kill plants. One rare kind of eagle is the bald eagle. It is a large bird with a dark brown and a white head. The bald eagle is the national symbol of some countries. When people see the bald eagle they are reminded that it is powerful and brave. These countries see themselves like the eagle.

1. **What is the main idea of this story?**
   a. Eagles are birds.
   b. Eagles are symbols of bravery and power.
   c. The bald eagle is brown and white.
2. **Where do eagles live?**
   Every continent except Antarctica
3. **The word "ancient" means:**
   a. long long ago
   b. brave
   c. powerful
4. **How do we know that eagles were symbols in ancient times?**
   Their pictures can be found on ancient buildings
5. **What is a bald eagle?**
   a bird with a brown and white head
6. **Why did the United States pick the bald eagle to be its symbol?**
   They are reminded that it is powerful and brave.

THINK AHEAD: Why do you think people like to hunt or capture eagles?

©1995 Kelley Wingate Publications, Inc.   9   KW 1014

Name _____ skill: comprehension

Flags

Flags are pieces of cloth that hang from poles, or something like a stick. We don't think of sticks and pieces of cloth as being very important. And yet, a flag is a very important symbol. A flag is a message that tells about a group of people. A white flag raised during a battle shows that one side is giving up. A flag placed on new land, like the moon, shows ownership. A flag flown over a city that has just been captured shows victory, or who won the battle. People fly the flags on certain days to show pride in their country. Each country has its own flag, kind of like its own coat of arms. Each flag is different and symbolizes what that country is about.

1. **What is the main idea of this story?**
   a. Flags are symbols of a whole group of people.
   b. The United States flag has stars and stripes.
   c. Flags send messages.
2. **What are flags?**
   a message
3. **Another word for "pole" is:**
   a. stick
   b. cloth
   c. flag
4. **Name three things that flags can tell us.**
   Giving up, ownership, victory
5. **What does the word "represent" mean?**
   a. flag
   b. mean
   c. stand for
6. **Why does each country have its own flag?**
   To symbolize what the country is about

THINK AHEAD: Design a flag that could symbolize your whole classroom.

©1995 Kelley Wingate Publications, Inc.   10   KW 1014

Name _____ skill: comprehension

Statue of Liberty

When you think of a symbol of the United States the Statue of Liberty is one that pops to mind. The statue was a gift to the American people from the French. France gave it to the United States in 1876 to celebrate the first 100 years of being a country. The Statue of Liberty is a woman holding a tablet, or book, in one hand and a torch, or light in the other. She is 150 feet tall and stands in New York Harbor. The Statue of Liberty was the first thing many people saw when they came to this country. Her gentle face welcomed them and her light showed them the way to a new life. Liberty is thought to be a symbol of strength mixed with warmness, a sort of mother that protects her children. She represents what the United States means to a lot of people.

1. **What is the main idea of this story?**
   a. Many people have seen the Statue of Liberty.
   b. The Statue of Liberty is a female.
   c. The Statue of Liberty is one symbol of the United States.
2. **Who gave the Statue of Liberty to the United States?**
   France
3. **What is the Statue of Liberty?**
   a symbol
4. **The word "tablet" means:**
   a. light
   b. book
   c. statue
5. **What does the statue symbolize?**
   Strength mixed with warmness
6. **How tall is the Statue of Liberty?**
   150 feet

THINK AHEAD: Use the library to find out more about the Statue of Liberty. What is the tablet she is holding? Why does she have a crown on her head?

©1995 Kelley Wingate Publications, Inc.   11   KW 1014

Answer Key

Name _____ skill: comprehension

Liberty Bell

In 1753 the United States was not a country yet. It was still ruled by England. However, many people wanted to break away from England and become a new country. That year the Liberty Bell was made and hung in the Pennsylvania State House. On the bell was written, "Proclaim Liberty throughout all the Land". These words mean that liberty, or freedom, was what the American people wanted. In 1776 the Declaration of Independence was written and the Liberty Bell was rung on July 4th to celebrate. The bell was hidden during the war against England. It had become a symbol of freedom for the American people, and they did not want the English to take it away. In 1846 the bell was brought out of hiding to be rung once again. A tiny crack in the bell opened up and it could not be rung. The bell is still quiet, but it stands on display in Philadelphia as a symbol of the struggle, or fight, for freedom.

1. What is the main idea of this story?
   a. The Liberty Bell symbolizes the fight for freedom. *(circled)*
   b. The Liberty Bell is cracked and cannot ring.
   c. The Americans fought the English for freedom.
2. In what year was the Liberty Bell made?

   1753
3. The word "liberty" means:
   a. country
   b. fight
   c. freedom *(circled)*
4. What is written on the Liberty Bell?

   "Proclaim Liberty throughout all the land"
5. Why was the Liberty Bell rung on July 4, 1776?

   To celebrate the Declaration of Independence.
6. What is another word for "fight"?
   a. struggle *(circled)*
   b. freedom
   c. liberty

THINK AHEAD: If the Liberty Bell had been captured by the English during the war, how would the American people have felt? Why?

©1995 Kelley Wingate Publications, Inc.   12   KW 1014

Name _____ skill: comprehension

Uncle Sam

Uncle Sam is a cartoon character who was first seen in the papers in 1812. The United States was fighting the British and many people were not happy about it. It was not proper, or right, to poke fun at the President so someone made up Uncle Sam. Uncle Sam is a tall, thin man with long white hair and a beard. He is usually dressed in a coat covered with stars, striped pants, and a top hat with stars and stripes on it. He symbolized the politics, or government, of the United States. Uncle Sam became a way of poking fun at the government without naming any one person as the problem. During World War II, Uncle Sam became a good guy. He was put on posters and reminded people of how they could help the country during the war. Today Uncle Sam can still be found in political cartoons.

1. What is the main idea of this story?
   a. Uncle Sam is a symbol of the United States government. *(circled)*
   b. Uncle Sam is a cartoon character.
   c. Cartoons poke fun at the government.
2. In what year did Uncle Sam first show up?

   1812
3. The word "proper" means:
   a. government
   b. correct or right *(circled)*
   c. politics
4. What does Uncle Sam look like?

   Tall, thin, white hair, a beard
5. What does Uncle Sam symbolize?

   The politics, or government of the US.
6. When did Uncle Sam become a good symbol?

   During World War II

THINK AHEAD: Why is it all right to poke fun at a cartoon, but not a person in the government?

©1995 Kelley Wingate Publications, Inc.   13   KW 1014

Name _____ skill: comprehension

Peace Pipe

A peace pipe was a large pipe with a bowl for burning tobacco, a plant for smoking. They were usually made of clay, stone, or wood and were decorated in many ways. The Native Americans used peace pipes at meetings. The pipes were more than tools to smoke tobacco. They were symbols that meant a lot to the people who used them. Indians believed the smoke was a way to send messages to the spirit world, a way to ask for help with problems. When soldiers or traders came into camp the Indians might bring out the peace pipe. The two groups would sit down together in a circle. Each person took a puff and passed it around the circle. The pipe became a symbol of friendship among those who smoked it together. Peace pipes were strong symbols, thought to be charms with the power to unite people.

1. What is the main idea of this story?
   a. Peace pipes were a way to smoke tobacco.
   b. Native Americans used peace pipes.
   c. Peace pipes were symbols of friendship. *(circled)*
2. What was a peace pipe used for?

   Symbols of peace
3. The word "tobacco" means:
   a. a large pipe
   b. a plant that can be smoked *(circled)*
   c. a circle of friendship
4. What did the Native Americans believe about smoke?

   It sends messages to the spirit world.
5. How were peace pipes used?

   They were passed around a circle.
6. If a Native American brought out a peace pipe, what did it mean?

   Friendship

THINK AHEAD: What symbols do we use today to show that we want to be friendly?

©1995 Kelley Wingate Publications, Inc.   14   KW 1014

Name _____ skill: comprehension

Animals

often been used to symbolized special ideas. Knights chose to put to symbolize bravery. Chinese kings used the dragon to symbolize animals to help describe, or tell about, how people behave. We as a mouse. People can be quick as a rabbit, low as a snake, or Many times we are hungry as a bear or have the memory of an elephant. Sports teams also choose names of different animals to symbolize themselves. Falcons are smart birds that fly very fast. Dolphins are graceful and smart. Buffaloes are big and hard to move. Colts can run fast and avoid (stay away from) getting caught. Animals can be used to symbolize the many different ways that people behave.

1. What is the main idea of this story?
   a. Animals can symbolize how people behave. *(circled)*
   b. A dragon symbolizes power.
   c. Sports teams use animal names.
2. What animal could we be as stubborn as?

   a mule
3. The word "describe" means:
   a. to tell about *(circled)*
   b. stay away from
   c. graceful
4. Why do sports teams often choose the name of a brave or fast animal?

   to symbolize how they play
5. What word means "to stay away from"?
   a. memory
   b. buffalo
   c. avoid *(circled)*
6. What is a person like if he is described as a mouse, snake, or bear/

   quiet, low, and hungry

THINK AHEAD: Can you think of three more animals that symbolize a human behavior?

©1995 Kelley Wingate Publications, Inc.   15   KW 1014

Answer Key

Name _____ skill: comprehension

Riddles

Twenty white horses upon a red hill.
Now they chomp. Now they stomp. Now they stand still.
What am I?

The words above make a riddle. It tells about white horses stomping and standing still. But riddles have a hidden meaning. Can you guess what the riddle is talking about? It is teeth! There are twenty white teeth in your mouth. The red hill is your gums. As you talk they move up and down as if they are chomping and stomping. When you finish talking they "stand still". Riddles give a symbolic meaning to things. Riddles have been used for thousands of years. In ancient times wise people would often answer questions with a riddle. It was believed that knowledge was precious, or of great value, and should not be given to people who were not very smart. If a person could figure out a riddle, he was smart enough to know the answer.

1. What is the main idea of this story?
   a. Riddles were used as symbols.
   b. Riddles have been used for many years.
   c. Riddles are hard to figure out.
2. What is a riddle?
   They give symbolic meanings to things
3. The word "precious" means:
   a. a lot of money
   b. meaning
   c. valuable
4. How long have riddles been used?
   For thousands of years
5. Why did wise people speak in riddles instead of giving an answer?
   because knowledge was precious
6. What are teeth called in the riddle?
   twenty white horses

THINK AHEAD: Make up a riddle about something you have or use every day.

©1995 Kelley Wingate Publications, Inc.   16   KW 1014

Name _____ skill: comprehension

Birthstones

Each month of the year has its own special gemstone, or valuable stone. People who wear their birthstone are believed to have special luck. Birthstones date back to about 3250 years ago. Moses was the leader of the people of Israel. His brother, Aaron was a high priest. Aaron wore a breastplate, or armor for the chest, that had twelve stones on it. Each stone stood for one of the twelve tribes, or groups of Israel. Over the years the stones became symbols of the twelve months of the year. Each stone is thought to bring special luck. For example, the diamond is supposed to bring happiness. The pearl brings wealth or health. Here is a list of the birthstones for each month.

January - garnet	February - amethyst	March - aquamarine
April - diamond	May - emerald	June - pearl
July - ruby	August - peridot	September - sapphire
October - opal	November - topaz	December - turquoise

1. What is the main idea of this story?
   a. Birthstones are gemstones.
   b. Birthstones are symbols of good luck.
   c. Birthstones are over 3000 years old.
2. What is a gemstone?
   a valuable stone
3. What did the first twelve gemstones symbolize?
   the twelve tribes of Isreal
4. Who wore the twelve gemstones on a breastplate:
   a. Moses
   b. Aaron
   c. a priest
5. What is a breastplate?
   Armor for the chest
6. Which birthstone is yours?

THINK AHEAD: Use the library to find out what luck your birthstone is believed to bring.

©1995 Kelley Wingate Publications, Inc.   17   KW 1014

Name _____ skill: comprehension

Colors

Colors are sometimes used to give meanings to things. When you see the color red, you think of things that are hot or dangerous. Fire engines are red so they can be easily seen and people will get out of their way. A red light or red sign on the street means to stop. Green is a color we use to mean "go". A green light on the street tells us it is safe to continue, or go on. Green signs in store windows mean the store is open. The color white can mean two things. If a white flag is held up it means surrender, or giving up. White can also mean that something is pure, or clean. Yellow or orange make people feel sunny, warm, or happy. Those are the colors used to symbolize the sun. Blue is a cool color, reminding us of water or ice. The use of colors help give meaning to things we see.

1. What is the main idea of this story?
   a. Colors can symbolize feelings or ideas.
   b. Red means stop.
   c. Blue is cold like ice.
2. What messages do we get when we see the color red?
   Things are hot or dangerous
3. The word "continue" means:
   a. stop
   b. go on
   c. be careful
4. What two things can the color white mean?
   Surrender or pure
5. What word means "to give up"?
   a. surrender
   b. continue
   c. pure
6. Why do the colors yellow or orange make us feel warm or happy?
   They remind us of the sun.

THINK AHEAD: What do some other colors (black, purple, brown) mean to you?

©1995 Kelley Wingate Publications, Inc.   18   KW 1014

Name _____ skill: comprehension

Producers

All living things will die without food. Food provides energy which is needed for growth and change. Animals must find food to eat. Plants do not need to look for food. They can make their own food by using energy from the sun. Plants have a special green chemical called chlorophyll that traps the suns energy. The energy is used to make food from the water and minerals the plant gets through its roots. This process is called photosynthesis. Living things, like plants, that can make their own food are called producers. Living things that cannot produce their own food depend on producers. They need the producers to get energy. Cows and sheep eat grass to get their energy. People eat vegetables, fruits, and nuts to get some of their energy. Because producers can make their own food, they do not need to depend on other living things. All plants are producers.

1. What is the main idea of this story?
   a. Plants are producers.
   b. People eat plants.
   c. Chlorophyll traps energy from the sun.
2. What are producers?
   Plants that can make their own food
3. The word depend means:
   a. make food
   b. need
   c. get energy
4. What is chlorophyll?
   a. A process that changes energy to food
   b. The process of growing
   c. A green chemical that traps energy from the sun
5. What is photosynthesis?
   Plants making food from water and minerals
6. Why do other living things need producers?
   They need food

THINK AHEAD: What would happen if there were no producers?

©1995 Kelley Wingate Publications, Inc.   19   KW 1014

Answer Key

Consumers

Animals need energy from food. They use the energy to grow and stay alive. Unlike plants, animals cannot make their own food. They must consume, or eat, food to get the energy they need. There are three kinds of consumers. Herbivores are animals that eat only plants. Cows, deer, goats, and mice are some herbivores. They eat the plants and get the energy the plant has stored from the sun. Another consumer is the carnivore. Carnivores are animals that eat only other animals. Lions, wolves, ferrets, and spiders are carnivores. They hunt or trap other animals and eat them to get their energy. The third type of consumer is the omnivore, which eats both plants and animals. Humans, bears, raccoons, and turtles are some omnivores.

1. **What is the main idea of this story?**
   a. Animals that cannot make their own food are consumers.
   b. Humans are consumers.
   c. Carnivores are consumers.
2. **What are the three types of consumers?**
   Herbivores, carnivores, and omnivores.

3. **What word means "eat"?**
   a. carnivore
   b. energy
   c. consume
4. **What do herbivores eat?**
   only plants
5. **What type of consumer eats both plants and animals?**
   Omnivore
6. **What do carnivores eat?**
   meat

THINK AHEAD: Find three pictures of animals that are eating. Identify them as herbivore, carnivore, or omnivore.

©1995 Kelley Wingate Publications, Inc.   20   KW 1014

Food Chain

The sun shines down on the earth. In a pond the small plant, algae, gathers the sun's energy and grows. A water flea stops to eat some of the algae. The energy now passes from the plant to the water flea. The flea passes a frog who flicks his tongue and has the flea for lunch. The energy from the flea is passed on to the frog. Later in the day, a snake eats the frog. The energy is passed on to the snake. That night an owl swoops down and catches the snake for dinner. Once again, energy is transferred from one animal to another. This story shows how energy from the sun is passed on to larger and larger animals. As each animal hunts and eats, preys on, smaller animals they gather more energy. The passing on of energy from one living thing to another is called a food chain.

1. **What is the main idea of this story?**
   a. Animals eat each other.
   b. The food chain is how animals get energy.
   c. Living things need energy.
2. **What is algae?**
   a small plant
3. **Where does a plant get its energy?**
   From the sun

4. **How does energy get from one living thing to another?**
   Through the food chain

5. **What does the word "transfer" mean?**
   a. to hunt and eat
   b. to pass on
   c. a small plant
6. **What is a food chain?**
   a. the things we eat
   b. the path of energy as is passes from one living thing to another
   c. a frog eating algae

THINK AHEAD: What did you eat for dinner last night? Pick one thing and trace your food chain back to the sun.

©1995 Kelley Wingate Publications, Inc.   21   KW 1014

Scavengers

Some consumers do not catch or kill their food. They get their food from plants or animals that have already died. These animals are called scavengers. A hyena is a scavenger. It will wait while the lion eats what it kills. When the lion is finished the hyena moves in and takes what is left. Vultures are also scavengers. They circle in the sky and look for animals that have died. When no other animals are near, the vulture will land and pick at the remains. One scavenger that lives in the water is a crab. Crabs will eat the remains of dead fish they may find. Scavengers need energy, just like all living things but they do not prey on animals. They eat what is left from the hunt of other animals.

1. **What is the main idea of this story?**
   a. A hyena is a scavenger.
   b. Crabs eat dead fish.
   c. Scavengers eat animals that are already dead.
2. **Are scavengers producers or consumers?**
   Consumers
3. **How does a hyena get its food?**
   It is a scavenger
4. **How does a vulture get its food?**
   The circle in the sky looking for dead animals.
5. **What are the three examples of scavengers given in the story?**
   Hyena, vulture, crab.

6. **How do scavengers help nature?**
   They eat what is left from the hunt.

THINK AHEAD: Name two other animals that are scavengers.

©1995 Kelley Wingate Publications, Inc.   22   KW 1014

Parasites

Some animals get their food by living in or on other living things. These animals do not kill the animal they live on, but they may harm or irritate them. Animals that live on or in other animals are called parasites. A flea will live on a dog, cat, or other animal. The flea gets its food by sucking the other animals blood. The dog or cat it lives on is called the host. The blood the flea takes is not enough to harm the host, but the flea causes the host to itch and be uncomfortable. Some worms are parasites. A tapeworm lives inside the body of animals. It gets its food from food the host has eaten. The tapeworm can take so much of the food (energy) that the host becomes very sick. There are even some plants that can be parasites. Mistletoe and some types of ferns live on trees, taking food and water from the them.

1. **What is the main idea of this story?**
   a. Parasites live on or in other living things.
   b. A flea is a parasite.
   c. Parasites can make the host sick.
2. **How does a flea get food?**
   Sucking another animals blood.
3. **Where does a tapeworm live?**
   Inside the body of an animal.
4. **What is a parasite?**
   Animals that live on or in another animal.
5. **What does the word "host" mean?**
   a. an animal that lives on other living things
   b. the animal a parasite lives on
   c. mistletoe
6. **What kinds of plants can be parasites?**
   Mistletoe and some types of ferns.

THINK AHEAD: Find another example of a parasite.

©1995 Kelley Wingate Publications, Inc.   23   KW 1014

Answer Key

Name _____ skill: comprehension

Mutualism

Some living things have special relationships with each other. They help each other get food. A sea anemone will sting most fish, but it will not hurt a clown fish. When enemies are close, the clown fish will hide near the sea anemone and be protected. In turn, the clown fish drops some of its food which helps feed the sea anemone. The sea anemone and the hermit crab can also help each other. Sometimes the sea anemone will attach itself to the shell of the hermit crab. The sea anemone rides on the shell and has a greater chance of finding food. Often it will eat food that the hermit crab cannot finish. The sea anemone helps the crab, too. The crab is hidden, or camouflaged, so its enemies will not see it. In this way the crab and anemone help each other survive, or stay alive. This relationship of helping each other is called mutualism.

1. What is the main idea of this story?
   a. Clown fish help sea anemones.
   b. Crabs and sea anemones live together.
   c. When animals help each other the relationship is called mutualism.
2. How does the sea anemone help the clown fish?

   It protects the clown fish.

3. How does the clown fish help the sea anemone?

   It gives it some of its food.

4. What is Mutualism?

   The relationship of helping each other.

5. What does the word "camouflage" mean?
   a. to hunt and eat
   b. to help each other
   c. to hide or disguise
6. What does the word "survive" mean?
   a. to stay alive
   b. a relationship
   c. sea anemone

THINK AHEAD: Can you find another example of mutualism?

©1995 Kelley Wingate Publications, Inc.   24   KW 1014

Name _____ skill: comprehension

Rocks

Rocks are everywhere we go. There are rocks in the dirt. There are small rocks, or pebbles, on beaches, in driveways, and on playgrounds. There are giant rocks in mountains and layers of rock under the dirt. What makes a rock? Rocks, like water, have a cycle, or pattern that repeats itself. Wind and water break large rocks into small pieces no bigger than sand. These pieces are called sediment. Over time sediment gets pressed down in the ground and becomes layers of rock. As the rock gets pressed harder it can become heated by the core of the earth and will finally melt. The melted rock, called magma, can be pushed out of volcanoes. When magma reaches the surface of the earth it is called lava. The lava cools and becomes rock that will be broken down by the wind and water. This pattern is called the rock cycle.

1. What is the main idea of this story?
   a. Rocks change, and the pattern is called the rock cycle.
   b. Sediment gets pressed into layers of rock.
   c. There are rocks all around us.
2. What are pebbles?

   Small rocks.

3. Sediment is :
   a. layers of rock
   b. small pieces of rock
   c. melted rock
4. What is lava?
   a. layers of rock
   b. small pieces of rock
   c. melted rock
5. In the rock cycle, what happens to sediment?

   Over time it is pressed down and becomes rock.

6. What causes rock to melt into magma?

   The heat at the core of the earth.

THINK AHEAD: Draw a picture of the rock cycle.

©1995 Kelley Wingate Publications, Inc.   25   KW 1014

Name _____ skill: comprehension

Minerals

The earth is full of chemicals. Some chemicals that lay deep in the earth get pressed together to form a solid that we call minerals. Diamonds, emeralds, gold, and quartz are minerals. We can tell what the minerals are by looking at some of their characteristics: color, hardness, and shape. Minerals come in many colors. Pure quartz is white. Often other chemicals mix with quartz and give it a pink or black color. When the pink, white, and black quartz are rubbed against a special tile they all leave the same color. This color helps tell us the mineral is quartz. Other minerals will leave a different color that tells what they are. Minerals range from hard to soft. Some minerals can be scratched with a fingernail. Diamonds are so hard only another diamond can scratch them. Each mineral also has its own atom pattern, or shape. As a mineral grows, the atom pattern guides the shape the mineral will take. No matter how large or small the mineral is, the shape will always be the same.

1. What is the main idea of this story?
   a. Minerals are pressed chemicals.
   b. Minerals are identified by color, hardness, and shape.
   c. Diamonds and gold are minerals.
2. Name four common minerals.

   diamonds, emerals, gold, and quartz

3. Some minerals come in different colors. How can you tell what mineral it is?

   rubbing against a special tile

4. Are all minerals hard? Explain.

   No, they range from hard to soft

5. How does a mineral get its shape?

   from its atom pattern

6. What is a mineral?

   Chemicals pressed together to form a solid

THINK AHEAD: Put any six objects in a row. Arrange them from softest to hardest.

©1995 Kelley Wingate Publications, Inc.   26   KW 1014

Name _____ skill: comprehension

Inside the Earth

What is inside the earth? Scientists believe the earth is a lot like a hard-boiled egg. The egg has a thin shell, a soft thick white layer, and a round yolk in the middle. The earth has a thin shell called the crust. It is about 8 to 32 kilometers deep. The crust is made of dirt, rocks, and minerals. Below the crust lies the mantle, a softer layer like the egg white. The mantle is much thicker than the crust and is very hot. The heat from this layer of the earth melts rocks that are at the bottom of the crust. The mantle is so hot that it pushes against the crust. Sometimes the melted rock pushes through the crust, causing volcanoes. No one has ever seen the mantle, but scientists learn about it by studying volcanoes and earthquakes. The very center of the earth, the part that is like the egg yolk, is called the core. Scientists believe that the core is about twice, or two times, as hot as the mantle. They think the core is made of the minerals nickel and iron.

1. What is the main idea of this story?
   a. The earth is shaped like an egg.
   b. Scientists believe the earth has three layers.
   c. The core of the earth is very hot.
2. What is the earth's crust?

   The thin crust made of dirt, rocks, and minerals

3. The mantle is:
   a. hot melted rock
   b. the thin outer layer of the earth
   c. made of nickel and iron
4. What layer of the earth causes volcanoes?

   the mantle

5. The core is:
   a. hot melted rock
   b. the thin outer layer of the earth
   c. made of nickel and iron
6. Which layer of the earth is the hottest?

   The core

THINK AHEAD: Draw a diagram of the earth's three layers.

©1995 Kelley Wingate Publications, Inc.   27   KW 1014

Answer Key

Volcanoes

The earth's mantle is so hot it melts rocks. The melted rock is called magma. Pressure inside the earth pushes the magma to the crust. Most of the time the magma cools in the crust, turning into layers of hard rock. Sometimes the magma finds a crack in the earth's crust. It pushes out of the opening and reaches the surface, or the outside, of the earth. Magma that reaches the surface is called lava. When lava flows from the crust it is called a volcano. If the lava has a lot of gas and water trapped in it, it will erupt or explode out of the crack. Lava with only a little water and gas will not erupt. This lava is thin and flows quietly from the cracks. As the lava cools it hardens to form rocks. Sometimes the lava will pile up around the opening of the volcano. It builds up to form a volcanic mountain.

1. What is the main idea of this story?
   a. Melted rock is called magma.
   b. Lava flows from volcanoes.
   c. Volcanoes are cracks in the earth where lava comes out.
2. What is magma?

   Melted rock
3. What happens to most of the magma when it reaches the crust?

   It cools
4. What is lava?
   a. magma that reaches the earth's surface
   b. a hard rock
   c. a crack in the earth's crust
5. What does lava do when it erupts?

   It explodes out of cracks in the earth's surface.
6. How are volcanic mountains formed?

   Lava piles up around the opening of a volcano.

THINK AHEAD: Draw a picture of a volcano. Label the lava, magma, and volcanic mountain.

Earthquakes

The inner layers of the earth are very hot. The heat causes pressure, pushing against the earth's crust. Cracks in the crust are called faults. Pressure from inside the earth can cause the crust along a fault to shift, or move. When the crust moves, it causes vibrations (a quick movement forward and backward) that shake the surface of the earth. These vibrations are called earthquakes. There are many earthquakes every day, but they are mild and we do not feel them. Sometimes earthquakes are very strong, shaking the earth so hard they can make buildings fall apart. Scientists measure earthquakes with a special machine called a seismograph. The seismograph shows us how big the vibrations are. Scientists rate the movement on a scale from one to ten. "One" means the earthquake is mild. The stronger the earthquake, the higher the number. Keeping records of earthquakes helps scientists understand more about them.

1. What is the main idea of this story?
   a. Inside the earth is very hot.
   b. Movement of the earth's crust is called an earthquake.
   c. A seismograph measures earthquakes.
2. Another word for a crack in the earth's crust is:
   a. seismograph
   b. pressure
   c. fault
3. What causes earthquakes?

   Movement in the crust of the earth caused by heat pressure
4. What is a vibration?

   A quick movement forward and backward.
5. How do scientists measure and learn more about earthquakes?

   They use a seismograph
6. What do you know about an earthquake that is rated "one"?

   It is mild

THINK AHEAD: What do you think would happen in your city or town if a earthquake rated nine shook the earth?

How Air is Warmed

The earth is surrounded by a layer of air. This layer of air is called the atmosphere. In some places, like a desert, the air feels very warm. In other places, perhaps near a lake, the air feels cooler. What makes the air warm or cool? The sun warms the air, but not as you might think. You become warm when you sit in the sun. That is because you absorb, or take in, the heat from the sun. All objects on the earth absorb sunlight. Darker objects absorb more heat than light colored objects. Water does not absorb as much heat as land. Air does not absorb heat this way because it has no color and the sunlight passes right through it. Things that do absorb the sunlight become very warm and radiate, or give off some of the heat. Think about how it feels to stand next to an oven that has been turned on. The air near the oven feels warm. The heat from the oven radiates and warms the air near it. Air near cities is warmer because the buildings absorb and radiate a lot of heat. Air over water is cooler than air over land because water absorbs and radiates less heat than land.

1. What is the main idea of this story?
   a. Air surrounds the earth.
   b. Air is warmed by objects that radiate heat.
   c. Cities absorb a lot of heat.
2. What is the atmosphere?

   The layer of air surrounding the earth
3. How does air become warm?

   From objects that radiate heat
4. The word "absorb" means:
   a. to take in
   b. to heat
   c. to give off
5. What does the word "radiate" mean?
   a. to take in
   b. to heat
   c. to give off
6. Why is it cooler near an ocean than in a city?

   Water absorbs less heat than land and buildings.

THINK AHEAD: Why do you think water absorbs less heat than land?

Atmosphere

The earth is surrounded by a layer of air that we call the atmosphere. The atmosphere is made of a mixture of gases and small solid particles, or pieces of things (like dust). Oxygen and nitrogen are important gases in the air. All plants and animals need oxygen to live. Plants use nitrogen to make their food. Water vapor is another gas in the air. Water vapor is what makes much of our weather - rain and snow. Without this gas the earth would be too dry for plants to grow. Ozone is a gas that can be found in the top layers of the atmosphere. This gas screens out harmful rays of energy that come from the sun. We use air in other ways, too. Without air, birds and planes could not fly. We could not blow up balloons or bicycle tires without air. The atmosphere is very important to our lives.

1. What is the main idea of this story?
   a. Air helps us in many ways.
   b. Ozone keeps harmful energy away.
   c. Planes need air to fly.
2. What is in the air we breathe?

   Gases and small solid particles.
3. The word "particle" means:
   a. gases
   b. small pieces
   c. vapor
4. What are the two gases plants and animals need to breathe?

   Oxygen and nitrogen
5. What gas protects the earth from harmful sun rays?

   Ozone
6. How does water vapor affect the earth?

   It makes up much of our weather such as rain and snow.

THINK AHEAD: Make a list of six ways we use air.

Answer Key

Orbit of Planets

A planet is a large object that orbits, or moves around the sun. There are nine planets that orbit our sun. Mercury, Venus, Earth, and Mars are the four planets closest to the sun. They are called the rocky planets because they are made mostly of rock. The other five planets are called the frozen planets. They are farthest from the sun and are made mostly of gases. Jupiter, Saturn, Uranus, Neptune, and Pluto are the frozen planets. The farther from the sun, the longer it takes for the planet to orbit the sun. This chart show how long it takes each planet to orbit the sun just once.

Mercury	88 days
Venus	225 days
Earth	365 days
Mars	2 years
Jupiter	12 years
Saturn	29 years
Uranus	84 years
Neptune	165 years
Pluto	248 years

1. What is the main idea of this story?
   a. Some planets are made of rock.
   b. Frozen planets are farthest from the sun.
   (c.) There are nine planets that revolve around the sun.
2. Name the rocky planets.
   Mercury, Venus, Earth, and Mars
3. Name the frozen planets.
   Jupiter, Saturn Uranus, Neptune, and Pluto
4. What does "revolve" mean?
   a. made of gases
   (b) move in a circle
   c. turn slowly
5. How many years does it take for Jupiter to revolve around the sun?
   _12_
6. Why does Neptune take longer to revolve than Mars?
   Because it is farther away from the sun.

THINK AHEAD: Draw a picture of the sun and its nine planets. Label them.

©1995 Kelley Wingate Publications, Inc.   32   KW 1014

Space Probes

We learn about planets by observing, or studying them. Scientists use a telescope to see planets. A telescope is a special instrument that makes far away objects look bigger. Some planets are too far away to see clearly, even when we use a telescope. How can we learn about these planets? Scientists send special spacecraft called probes into space. Probes travel through space, coming close to other planets. Telescopes and cameras are in the probe to record everything they see. Probes also carry special instruments to examine the weather and soil on other planets. The information is sent back to the earth where scientists can study it. The first probe, the Mariner 2, was launched in 1962. It gave us information about the planet Venus. Since then scientists have sent over 25 probes into space. Each probe tells us even more about the planets so far from our earth.

1. What is the main idea of this story?
   (a.) Probes tell us about other planets.
   b. Telescopes help us to see other planets.
   c. Mariner 2 was the first space probe.
2. What is a telescope?
   an instrument that makes far away things look bigger
3. What is a probe?
   a space craft that travels through space to examine planets
4. What information about other planets can a probe gather?
   weather and soil
5. What does the word "observe" mean?
   a. a special instrument
   (b.) to study
   c. probe
6. What special equipment do probes carry?
   telescopes and cameras

THINK AHEAD: Why do scientists want to know more about other planets?

©1995 Kelley Wingate Publications, Inc.   33   KW 1014

Holidays

The word holiday comes from "holy day" which is any day set aside to celebrate, or remember, something special. The holiday may be a time to remember indepence or it may be a time to remember people important to our history. Some holidays are to celebrate religious events like Easter, Christmas, Yom Kippur, or Chanukah. Food is often a big part of holidays. We think of turkey with Thanksgiving, eggs and candy with easter, and chocolate hearts with Valentines. Some holidays, like Ash Wednesday and Yom Kippur, are celebrated by fasting, or not eating at all. Each holiday has special customs, or traditions, that go along with it. We watch parades and fireworks, give gifts and cards, eat too much or not at all, and play hard or just rest. Whatever holiday we celebrate, the most important thing we do is feel a sense of belonging as we share with others.

1. The main idea of this story is:
   a. Food is a part of every holiday.
   (b.) Holidays are a time for sharing and belonging.
   c. Valentine's Day is a holiday.
2. Where does the word "holiday" come from?
   holy day
3. What does the word "fasting" mean?
   a. to go quickly
   b. to celebrate
   (c.) to not eat
4. What are some ways to celebrate holidays?
   watch parades and fireworks, give gifts and cards
5. What is the most important things about all holidays?
   we feel a sense of belonging as we share with others
6. What is another word for "remember"?
   a. religious
   (b.) celebrate
   c. tradition

Think Ahead: On another piece of paper, list all the holidays you can remember.

©1995 Kelley Wingate Publications, Inc.   34   KW 1014

Boxing Day

England celebrates a special holiday that is called Boxing Day. No, it does not have anything to do with a fight! Boxing Day is the first weekday after Christmas. If Christmas is on Tuesday, Wednesday is Boxing Day. If Christmas is on Friday, Saturday, or Sunday then Boxing Day will be on the next Monday. Now that you know when it is, let me tell you what it is! Boxing Day is a day set aside to thank people in service jobs. The English people gave gifts to mailmen, trash collectors, maids, or anyone who does jobs for them. But why call it Boxing Day? The name comes from the way the English prepare, or ready, the gifts. They are put into boxes before being wrapped up. Now you know about Boxing Day!

1. The main idea of this story is:
   (a.) Boxing Day honors service people.
   b. Presents are put into boxes then wrapped.
   c. Boxing Day is for mail carriers and maids.
2. In what country was Boxing Day first celebrated?
   England
3. What does the word "prepare" mean?
   a. to fight
   (b.) to ready
   c. to put in boxes
4. Who gets gifts on this holiday?
   People in service jobs.
5. When is Boxing Day celebrated?
   The first weekday after Christmas
6. Why is this holiday called Boxing Day?
   Because the presents are put into boxes.

Think Ahead: Why is it important to celebrate Boxing Day?

©1995 Kelley Wingate Publications, Inc.   35   KW 1014

Answer Key

Name _____ skill: comprehension

Australia Day

Australia Day is a holiday that honors Captain Arthur Phillip, the English founder of Sydney, the capital city. Captain Phillip came to Australia in 1788 to start a prison for England. One of the prisoners was an architect, who helped design the city. Sydney became a busy town that grew quickly. In 1890, Australia decided set aside a day to honor their country. They decided on January 26 and called it Victoria Day, after Queen Victoria of England. In 1935 Australia changed the name to Australia Day. It is now celebrated on the Monday after January 6, and remembers Captain Phillip.

1. The main idea of this story is:
   a. Australia Day is a day to honor Australia.
   b. Captain Phillip founded Sydney.
   c. In 1935 Victoria Day was changed to Australia Day.
2. Why did Captain Phillip come to Australia?

   He came to start a prison

3. What does the word "architect" mean?
   a. prisoners
   b. a person who designs buildings
   c. the queen of England
4. When did Australia first set aside a day for their country?

   1890

5. What is Australia Day celebrated?

   The first Monday after January 6

Think Ahead: List all the holidays you can remember.

©1995 Kelley Wingate Publications, Inc.   36   KW 1014

Name _____ skill: comprehension

Groundhog Day

Each February 2nd many people want to know what the groundhog will do. A popular legend says that on February 2nd the groundhog comes out of his home. He has been hibernating, or sleeping there, all winter. If the day is sunny, he will see his shadow. The shadow scares him and he goes back into his hole. The groundhog will go back to sleep for six more weeks. That means that winter will stay for six more weeks! If February 2nd is a cloudy day the groundhog will not see his shadow. He will stay outside, meaning that spring has come. Folklore, or old stories, from Europe are much the same except the animal is usually a bear or badger.

1. The main idea of this story is:
   a. February 2nd is Groundhog Day.
   b. Legend says the groundhog tells us when spring arrives.
   c. Some people watch bears and badgers.
2. What does the groundhog do all winter?

   hibernate

3. What does the word "hibernate" mean?
   a. come out of a winter home
   b. tell stories
   c. sleep all winter
4. What happens if the groundhog sees his shadow?

   it will be winter for six more weeks

5. What happens if February 2nd is a cloudy day?

   the groundhog will not see his shadow
   and that means spring has come.
6. What animals do Europeans watch on February 2nd?

   a bear or badger

Think Ahead: On the back of this paper, list all the holidays you can remember.

©1995 Kelley Wingate Publications, Inc.   37   KW 1014

Name _____ skill: comprehension

Valentines Day

In ancient Rome February 15th was a special day. Boys would pull girls names from a love urn, or large vase. They began to send cards to girls they liked the day before, February 14th. The cards were anonymous, they did not sign them, and the girls had to guess who sent the cards. Romans became Christians, a kind of religion, and the church did not like this custom. The church said the Roman boys had to stop giving the cards, but they did not stop. The church finally said they could send the cards if they celebrated the day as Saint Valentine's Day. Saint Valentine was a Roman priest in the church. The day was renamed and is now celebrated in many parts of the world.

1. The main idea of this story is:
   a. Valentine's Day is a day to celebrate love.
   b. Christians did not like the custom of giving cards.
   c. Valentine's Day is celebrated everywhere.
2. What day was first celebrated by the Romans?

   February 15th

3. What does the word "urn" mean?
   a. to pull names
   b. a large vase
   c. to send cards
4. Why was the day named Saint Valentine's Day?

   It was named after a Roman priest.

5. What word means "not signed"?
   a. urn
   b. Valentine
   c. anonymous
6. What day do we celebrate Saint Valentine's?

   February 14th

Think Ahead: Why do you think most valentines have hearts on them?

©1995 Kelley Wingate Publications, Inc.   38   KW 1014

Name _____ skill: comprehension

Memorial Day

The United States has set aside a day to remember people who have died while serving their country. These people were in the armed services: the Navy, Army, Marines, Air Force, or Coast Guard. Their job is to protect our country. Many of them died in wars. The holiday is meant for us to honor those people. Memorial Day was first observed, or celebrated, on May 30, 1868. The Civil War had just ended but many soldiers had died. People put flowers on the graves of the soldiers to honor them. Today almost every state celebrates this holiday on the last Monday in May.

1. The main idea of this story is:
   a. Memorial Day is to remember people who died in wars.
   b. People died to protect our country
   c. Memorial Day is on May 30
2. Who do we remember on Memorial Day?

   People who were in the armed forces.

3. What does the word "observed" mean?
   a. to celebrate
   b. to do a job
   c. to end a war
4. What do people do on Memorial Day?

   Put flowers on the graves of
   soldiers to honor.
5. Name four parts of the armed services:

   Army, Navy, Marines, Air Force,
   Coast Guard
6. On what day do we celebrate Memorial Day?

   The last Monday in May

Think Ahead: What does your town do to celebrate Memorial Day?

©1995 Kelley Wingate Publications, Inc.   39   KW 1014

Answer Key

Independence Day

July 4th is an important holiday for the United States. It is our Independence Day. On July 4, 1776 the United States declared, or stated, that we were a country on our own. We would no longer be a part of England. Independent means to take care of yourself without help from others. That is why July 4th is called Independence Day. Every 4th of July the United States celebrates the beginning of our own country. There are parades, speeches, and lots of fireworks. People fly their flags to show they are proud of our country.

1. **The main idea of this story is:**
   a. The 4th of July is to celebrate the founding of our country *(circled)*
   b. We have parades on the 4th of July
   c. The 4th of July is for fireworks
2. **On what day do we celebrate our independence?**
   July 4th
3. **What word means "to state or say"?**
   a. declare *(circled)*
   b. celebrate
   c. fireworks
4. **What are some ways we celebrate Independence Day?**
   Parades, speeches and fireworks
5. **Who did the United States become independent from?**
   England
6. **What does the word "independent" mean?**
   a. holiday
   b. stated
   c. free and on your own *(circled)*

Think Ahead: What does your family do on the 4th of July?

Labor Day

Labor Day is a holiday that is celebrated everywhere in the United States. Labor means work. Labor Day is a day to celebrate the things we have worked for. We take a day off work and relax, or rest. It is a day to think about all the things we have worked hard to make or get. Most people take the day off and have fun. Europe began to celebrate workers on May 1. They call their holiday May Day. The United States and Canada celebrate their holiday on the first Monday in September.

1. **The main idea of this story is:**
   a. May Day is the same as Labor Day
   b. People have fun on Labor Day
   c. Labor Day is to celebrate what we have worked for *(circled)*
2. **On what day do we celebrate Labor Day?**
   The first Monday in September
3. **What does the word "relax" mean?**
   a. think
   b. rest *(circled)*
   c. work
4. **What two countries celebrate Labor Day?**
   Canada and the United States
5. **What does Europe call their labor day?**
   May day
6. **When do Europeans celebrate their labor day?**
   May 1st.

Think Ahead: What is the date of Labor Day this year?

Halloween

Halloween has been celebrated for hundreds of years. People used to think that witches and warlocks, male witches, came out on the night of October 31. People would protect, or save, themselves by dressing in scary costumes and lighting big fires. They believed the witches would be frightened away by the bright light and ugly costumes. Most people do not believe that any more, but they still celebrate Halloween. It has become a holiday that children enjoy. On October 31 they dress in costumes and go trick-or-treating. After dark the children ring doorbells and people give them candy. People enjoy playing tricks and scaring everybody. Now it is done for fun, not protection.

1. **The main idea of this story is:**
   a. Halloween is a fun and scary holiday. *(circled)*
   b. Halloween is for witches.
   c. Children get candy.
2. **On what day do we celebrate Halloween?**
   October 31st.
3. **What does the word "protect" mean?**
   a. to ask for candy
   b. to keep yourself safe *(circled)*
   c. to scare people
4. **Why did people dress up and light fires on Halloween long ago?**
   To scare witches and warlocks
5. **What is Halloween for now?**
   Fun
6. **What is another word for "male witch"?**
   a. Halloween
   b. protect
   c. warlock *(circled)*

Think Ahead: Draw a picture of the costume you will wear next Halloween.

Armistice Day

On November 11, 1918 World War I ended. The day was called Armistice Day. Armistice means a truce or agreement to stop fighting. In 1919 President Wilson said that Armistice Day would be celebrated to remember people who had died to protect their country. People who fought in wars are called veterans. Armistice Day would honor those veterans of the war. Every November 11 people fly flags and visit the graves of veterans. There are parades where veterans march so we can honor them. In 1954 the name Armistice Day was changed to Veterans Day. Now we honor the veterans from all the wars.

1. **The main idea of this story is:**
   a. Armistice Day was named by President Wilson.
   b. Armistice Day is to honor veterans of wars. *(circled)*
   c. November 11, 1918 World War I ended.
2. **What is Armistice Day?**
   The day World War I ended.
3. **What does the word "armistice" mean?**
   a. flags
   b. people who fought in wars
   c. a truce *(circled)*
4. **When was Armistice Day renamed?**
   1954
5. **Who do we honor on Armistice Day?**
   People who fought in wars.
6. **When do we celebrate Veterans Day?**
   November 11th.

Think Ahead: Find out how many wars the United States has been in since 1918.

Answer Key

Name _____   skill: comprehension

Thanksgiving

Thanksgiving is a holiday the United States celebrates on the fourth Thursday in November. It began in 1621 with the Pilgrims. They had come to America and had a very hard first year. Many people died because they were cold and did not have enough food. The second year they were here the Native Americans helped them. The Native Americans taught the Pilgrims how to grow corn and hunt for wild turkeys. That fall the Pilgrims had plenty of food to eat. They were very thankful. They celebrated their good year by praying and giving a big feast, or meal, that lasted three days. It was a time to thank the Indians for all their help. Many people kept the celebration every year. They give thanks for all the good things they have. In 1863, President Lincoln made Thanksgiving a national holiday, a holiday for the whole country.

1. The main idea of this story is:
   a. Thanksgiving is a time to celebrate what we are thankful for.
   b. Thanksgiving began in 1621.
   c. Thanksgiving is a time to eat a lot.
2. Who started Thanksgiving?
   The Pilgrims
3. What does the word "feast" mean?
   a. a big meal
   b. to be thankful
   c. Native Americans
4. In what year was the first Thanksgiving?
   1622
5. Why do people celebrate Thanksgiving today?
   To give thanks for all the good things.
6. What does "national holiday" mean?
   a. a religious holiday
   b. celebrate each year
   c. a holiday for the country

Think Ahead: Why do you think food is such an important part of Thanksgiving?

©1995 Kelley Wingate Publications, Inc.   44   KW 1014

Name _____   skill: comprehension

Chanukah

Chanukah is a Jewish festival that is celebrated in December. It is also called the Festival of Lights. Chanukah is a celebration that began in 165 B.C. The Jewish people had been forbidden to use their temple, place of worship. They fought to get the temple back. It is said that a when they went back to the temple they had only enough oil to burn their lamps for one day. A miracle, something impossible, happened and the oil lasted for eight days. During Chanukah one candle is lit each night for eight nights to remember the miracle. The eight candles are put in a candlestick called a Menorah. The Menorah has become a symbol, or sign of, Chanukah.

1. The main idea of this story is:
   a. Chanukah is a Jewish festival to remember a miracle.
   b. Eight candles are burned in December.
   c. The Menorah means it is Chanukah time.
2. In what year did Chanukah begin?
   165 B.C.
3. What does the word "temple" mean?
   a. a place of worship
   b. something impossible
   c. a candle holder
4. What miracle happened in the temple?
   The oil burned for eight days.
5. What is a Menorah?
   A type of candlestick
6. What word means about the same as "symbol"?
   a. impossible
   b. sign
   c. miracle

Think Ahead: Why do you think Chanukah is also called the Festival of Lights?

©1995 Kelley Wingate Publications, Inc.   45   KW 1014

Name _____   skill: comprehension

Christmas

Christmas is a religious holiday that is celebrated on December 25. It is a day set aside to remember the birth of Jesus Christ. In the year 274, the Roman emperor Aurelian declared this day to be the feast of the "Invincible Sun". Eastern churches picked January 6 as the day to celebrate because that is the day the three wise men reached Bethlehem, the city where Christ was born. Over time, the celebration became known as Epiphany and is celebrated from December 25 until January 6. This time is commonly called the Twelve Days. The four weeks before Christmas are called Advent. Advent used to be a quiet time to prepare for the feast of Christmas. During the last 100 years Christmas celebrations have slowly moved into Advent time. Christmas events now begin as early as Thanksgiving day.

1. The main idea of this story is:
   a. Christmas is a religious holiday that is celebrated for many days.
   b. The Christmas holiday begins on Thanksgiving.
   c. Epiphany is another name for Christmas.
2. In what year was Christmas first celebrated?
   274
3. What is another name for "Epiphany"?
   a. Advent
   b. the Twelve Days
   c. Aurelian
4. What was Christmas called when it first began?
   The feast of the "Invincible Sun"
5. What Roman emperor began the celebration?
   Aurelian
6. What is "Advent"?
   a. a religious holiday
   b. the Twelve Days of Christmas
   c. the four weeks before Christmas

Think Ahead: Why do you think the celebration of Christmas has slowly moved up to right after Thanksgiving?

©1995 Kelley Wingate Publications, Inc.   46   KW 1014

Name _____   skill: comprehension

Honoring Others

There are many holidays that are celebrated quietly. The country does not stop work to celebrate and there are no parades. These days are set aside to remember special groups of people. Secretaries are remembered on the last Wednesday in April. Mother's Day is the first Sunday in May. Father's Day is the third Sunday in June. Friendship Day is in August. A day to honor Grandparents is the second Sunday in September. On the third Saturday of October we honor those we love and call it Sweetest Day. These holidays are called civil holidays, days that the country remembers but does not make a big fuss over. On civil holidays we send cards, call people, and do nice things for those we are honoring.

1. The main idea of this story is:
   a. Mother's Day is in May.
   b. Everyone works on civil holidays.
   c. Civil holidays are days that we honor other people.
2. When do we celebrate Father's Day?
   The third Sunday in June
3. List three civil holidays we celebrate.
   Secretary's Day, Mother's Day, Father's Day, Friendship Day, Grandparent's Day, and Sweetest Day
4. On what day do we celebrate Grandparents Day?
   The second Sunday in September.
5. What month do we celebrate our friendships?
   August
6. What are some of the ways we celebrate civil holidays?
   Send cards, call people and do nice things.

Think Ahead: What does your family do to celebrate civil holidays?

©1995 Kelley Wingate Publications, Inc.   47   KW 1014

Answer Key

Greeting Cards

A greeting card is a printed message, or thought, that we send to other people. There is usually a picture on the front and the message inside the card. The custom of sending greeting cards can be traced back to about 500 B.C. when Egyptians sent written messages with their New Years gifts. Greeting cards also played an important part in the holiday of Valentines Day when people would send messages to their sweethearts. The first printed cards were found in Europe in the 1400's. People made woodcut prints, a design cut out of wood then painted and stamped on paper. Europeans sent these cards as New Years greetings. The modern greeting card became popular in the late 1800's because printing was quick and easy and cards could be mailed to people across the country. Today greeting cards can be found for civil and religious holidays, anniversaries, birthdays, and just about any occasion you can think of.

1. The main idea of this story is:
    a. Greeting cards have been around for over two thousand years.
    b. Greeting cards are a way of sending messages for special occasions.
    c. We send greeting cards on birthdays.
2. What does the word "message" mean?
    a. a greeting card
    b. a printed thought or feeling
    c. New Years gifts
3. When did people first send greeting cards to others?
   About 500 B.C.
4. Where were the first printed greeting cards found?
   Europe
5. How were the first printed greeting cards made?
   They were woodcut prints.
6. Why did cards become popular in the late 1800's?
   Because printing was quick and easy and cards could be mailed to people across the country

Think Ahead: On what occasions does your family exchange greeting cards?

©1995 Kelley Wingate Publications, Inc.   48   KW 1014

Nouns

Cloze is a reading exercise where some of the words are missing and you must put them back in. Read the story below. Some of the nouns have been taken out. Fill in the blanks with the words below the story.

Caitlin's Big Day

Caitlin counted her money one last time. It was all there. **Caitlin** had saved her extra **money** for the last five weeks. She had planned this day for a long **time** and now it was here! Caitlin carefully put the money in her **wallet**. She did not want to lose a single **penny**. Caitlin walked to Lee's house. Lee had saved her money, too. The **girls** walked to town. They went to the movie theater and bought two **tickets** for the show. Each girl bought a box of **popcorn** and a cold **soda**. They watched the **movie**, enjoying every minute of it. When the movie was over, Caitlin and Lee walked to the ice cream **store**. They had just enough money left for a hot fudge **sundae**. What a wonderful **day** it had been!

Caitlin day girls money movie penny popcorn
soda store sundae tickets time wallet

©1995 Kelley Wingate Publications, Inc.   49   KW 1014

Nouns

Cloze is a reading exercise where some of the words are missing and you must put them back in. Read the story below. Some of the nouns have been taken out. Fill in the blanks with the words below the story.

The Parade

Ryan and Evan were excited. **Today** they were going to the **circus** parade. The circus came to **town** every five years. The last **time** it was here Ryan and Evan had the **measles** and could not go. This time **they** were healthy and eager to see everything! Ryan had asked his father what kinds of **animals** they would see. Evan asked his mother to tell **him** about the circus acts. He wanted to know all about the dancing **bears** and tightrope walkers. Both **boys** had their cameras so they could take **pictures** of the things they liked best. Ryan and Evan were all dressed and ready to go. There was only one **problem**. The **parade** would not begin for three more **hours**!

animals bears boys circus him hours measles
parade pictures problem they time Today town

©1995 Kelley Wingate Publications, Inc.   50   KW 1014

Nouns

Cloze is a reading exercise where some of the words are missing and you must put them back in. Read the story below. Some of the nouns have been taken out. Fill in the blanks with the words below the story.

A Visitor

The teacher told the children to clear their desks. She had **something** important to tell **them**. The class buzzed with **whispers** as books and **pencils** were quickly stuffed into desks. They could tell that the **teacher** was excited and happy. Her cheeks glowed and her eyes sparkled as **she** watched them get ready. The **children** were finished in no time. They sat with their **hands** folded on their laps or desktops. Every **eye** was fixed on the teacher. What could be so important? The teacher cleared her **throat** and began. The class had an important **visitor** who was waiting in the **hall**. The **door** opened and in stepped a **man** dressed in a suit. It was the **leader** of their country! The class gasped in surprise.

children door eye hall hands man pencils leader
she something teacher them throat visitor whispers

©1995 Kelley Wingate Publications, Inc.   51   KW 1014

Answer Key

Name _____
skill: cloze

Verbs

Cloze is a reading exercise where some of the words are missing and you must put them back in. Read the story below. Some of the verbs have been taken out. Fill in the blanks with the words below the story.

A Paper Route

John has a job. Early each morning he __gets__ up and quickly __dresses__. He must be out of the house and on the job by five o'clock. John __delivers__ papers to the people in his neighborhood. He __arrives__ at the drugstore just in time to meet the paper truck. He must __count__ out 72 papers for his route. John carefully __folds__ each paper and __slides__ it into a plastic bag. When all his papers __are__ ready, John __loads__ them into the basket on his bicycle. Now the real work begins! John __pedals__ his bike through the neighborhood. He __tosses__ papers on front lawns or porches. John __is__ careful to leave the paper where the customer __likes__ to find it. John __feels__ good when he is __doing__ his job. He __knows__ that his job is important to many people.

are arrives count delivers doing dresses feels folds
gets is knows likes loads pedals slides tosses

Name _____
skill: cloze

Verbs

Cloze is a reading exercise where some of the words are missing and you must put them back in. Read the story below. Some of the verbs have been taken out. Fill in the blanks with the words below the story.

Nosy the Kitten

Nosy was a happy little kitten. She __had__ a mother who __loved__ her very much. She __lived__ in a warm house with many children. Nosy had everything a kitten could __want__. The only problem __was__ that Nosy was nosy! Just last week she had __played__ with a ball of yarn and got all __tangled__ up in it. One of the children __spent__ almost half an hour __unwrapping__ the yarn from her paws. This morning Nosy __saw__ a nest near the top of the maple tree. She __climbed__ up the tree to __see__ what was in the nest. It was not hard to __reach__ the high limb. __Getting__ down was not so easy. Nosy __looked__ down from the high branch and became dizzy. Now she is __stuck__ in the tree. What a nosy kitten!

climbed had Getting lived looked loved played reach
saw see spent stuck tangled unwrapping want was

Name _____
skill: cloze

Verbs

Cloze is a reading exercise where some of the words are missing and you must put them back in. Read the story below. Some of the verbs have been taken out. Fill in the blanks with the words below the story.

The Hungry Bear

Betsy bear was taking her winter nap in her den. She felt water __dripping__ on her nose. Drip. Drip. Drip. Betsy lazily __opened__ one eye and __looked__ up. The winter snow was __melting__. It was time to get up. Betsy __stretched__ her huge paws over her head. She __yawned__ a big yawn and sighed. It was so cozy in her den. She really didn't want to __wake__ up yet. Maybe she could __roll__ over and go back to __sleep__ for just a little while. Betsy settled back down and __closed__ her eyes. Suddenly she heard a loud __growling__ noise. Was that another bear? Betsy __sat__ up and looked around. There __was__ the noise again. She looked down at her tummy. The growl had __come__ from her! Betsy's tummy __knew__ it was time to get up and __find__ something to eat. Spring had arrived!

closed come dripping find growling knew looked melting
opened roll sat sleep stretched wake was yawned

Name _____
skill: cloze

Adjectives

Cloze is a reading exercise where some of the words are missing and you must put them back in. Read the story below. Some of the adjectives have been taken out. Fill in the blanks with the words below the story.

The Parrot

Sam knew just what he wanted for his birthday. Last week he had gone to __Mr. Brown's__ pet store to look at the __cute__ puppies in the __front__ window. Sam loved to rub their __soft__ ears and feel their __wet__ noses. But as he entered the store Sam heard a __loud__ squawk. Sam saw a __large__ wire cage near the back of the store. Inside the cage was the __prettiest__ bird he had ever seen. Mr. Brown told Sam that the bird was a parrot. The parrot had green and __yellow__ feathers, a __hooked__ beak, and __sharp__ claws on each toe. The __big__ bird looked at Sam and said, "Hello boy." Sam laughed and petted the bird's __funny__ feathers. He knew that the __beautiful__ bird was the __perfect__ gift for him. That is what he wanted for his birthday!

beautiful big cute front furry hooked large loud
Mr. Brown's perfect prettiest sharp soft wet yellow

Answer Key

Name _____ skill: cloze

Adjectives

Cloze is a reading exercise where some of the words are missing and you must put them back in. Read the story below. Some of the adjectives have been taken out. Fill in the blanks with the words below the story.

The Farm

Brandon had a great time last summer. He had spent __two__ weeks on his uncle's farm. Brandon lived in a __big__ city, so the farm was __new__ and different for him. Every morning the __old__ rooster stood on the __wooden__ fence rail and crowed at the __glowing__ sun. Brandon had __many__ chores to do before breakfast. He gathered the __brown__ eggs the hens had just laid. He gently reached under each __fat__ hen and carefully lifted out the __warm__ eggs. Then it was time to feed the __wooly__ sheep. After that it was time to give the horses __clean__ water to drink. Finally Brandon went back to the kitchen where he found __crisp__ bacon and __scrambled__ eggs waiting for him. He was __very__ hungry and __always__ ate a lot for breakfast. Life on the farm was lots of fun!

always big brown clean crisp fat glowing many new old scrambled two very warm wooden woolly

©1995 Kelley Wingate Publications, Inc.   56   KW 1014

Name _____ skill: cloze

Adjectives

Cloze is a reading exercise where some of the words are missing and you must put them back in. Read the story below. Some of the adjectives have been taken out. Fill in the blanks with the words below the story.

A Great Meal

This Thanksgiving I had the best meal ever! My mother baked a __fifteen__ pound turkey. The skin was a golden __brown__ color. The meat was so __juicy__ I had to use two napkins to keep my chin dry! The red __cranberry__ sauce was just __sweet__ enough for me. My sister liked the __mashed__ potatoes, but I liked the yams with __melted__ marshmallows on top. We had a jello salad that sat on __green__ lettuce leaves. The __hot__ rolls tasted so good I ate __four__ of them! But my favorite food was the __pumpkin__ pie with __whipped__ cream on top. I felt so full I could barely walk. After that __delicious__ meal, I found a __comfortable__ pillow and laid down. We watched a __football__ game and I fell __fast__ asleep. What a wonderful day!

brown comfortable cranberry delicious fast fifteen football four green hot juicy mashed melted pumpkin sweet whipped

©1995 Kelley Wingate Publications, Inc.   57   KW 1014

Name _____ skill: cloze

Cloze

Cloze is a reading exercise where some of the words are missing and you must put them back in. Read the story below. Every tenth word has been taken out. Fill in the blanks with the words you think will make sense.

A Popcorn Ball

My father took me to a baseball game today. The stands were crowded but we found our seats. __Dad__ was upset because we were almost at the end __of__ the stands. They were not good seats. I didn't __mind__ . I liked being with my dad, even if we __could__ not see the game very well. Dad settled down __and__ bought each of us a box of popcorn. The __popcorn__ was stale and cost too much money. Poor dad __was__ not having a very good day. The first batter __hit__ the ball. The ball popped into the air __and__ was coming into the stands. It was a home __run__ ! Dad stood up and the ball landed in his __box__ of popcorn. The popcorn and seats turned out to be pretty good after all!

and and box could Dad hit mind of popcorn run was

©1995 Kelley Wingate Publications, Inc.   58   KW 1014

Name _____ skill: cloze

Cloze

Cloze is a reading exercise where some of the words are missing and you must put them back in. Read the story below. Every tenth word has been taken out. Fill in the blanks with the words you think will make sense.

The Haunted House

It was a very dark night. The house looked scary standing under the shadowy old __oak__ trees. The four friends stood at the front gate. __No__ one wanted to be the first to step into __the__ yard. One of them pointed a flashlight at the __dark__ windows. They looked dusty and several of them were __broken__ . The house sure looked haunted, even though none of __them__ believed that it was. Not one of the boys __said__ a word. Each boy was frightened but did not __want__ the others to know. An owl hooted from the __top__ of the largest oak tree. The boys all jumped __but__ did not run away. The tallest boy cleared his __throat__ but did not speak. Were they really going to go into that spooky old place?

broken but dark No oak said the them throat top want

©1995 Kelley Wingate Publications, Inc.   59   KW 1014

©1995 Kelley Wingate Publications, Inc.   121   CD-3711

Answer Key

Name _____   skill: cloze

Cloze

Cloze is a reading exercise where some of the words are missing and you must put them back in. Read the story below. Every eighth word has been taken out. Fill in the blanks with the words you think will make sense.

Hunting For a Rainbow

Maggie pulled the rubber boots on over her shoes. She slid into her yellow raincoat and **snapped** the front closed. This was just the **weather** she had been hoping for. The sky **was** a light grey with bits of blue **peeking** through. Maggie knew that this time she **would** find what she was looking for. She **stepped** out the door and opened the big **red** umbrella over her head. The light rain **danced** on the rounded top and quickly slid **down** the sides. Her boots splashed through the **puddles** as Maggie walked through them. The rain **had** almost stopped so Maggie hurried faster. She **reached** the top of the hill and looked. **Sure** enough, this time she had found it! Beyond the hill was a beautiful rainbow sparkling in the sun.

danced down had peeking puddles reached red snapped stepped Sure was weather would

©1995 Kelley Wingate Publications, Inc.   60   KW 1014

Name _____   skill: cloze

Cloze

Cloze is a reading exercise where some of the words are missing and you must put them back in. Read the story below. Every eighth word has been taken out. Fill in the blanks with the words you think will make sense.

Banana Split

Have you ever made a banana split? It is easy to do. First you **need** a big bowl. Peel a banana and **cut** it in half from one end to **the** other. The cut banana goes in the **bottom** of the bowl. Next, put three scoops **of** ice cream on top of the banana. **Cover** each scoop of ice cream with your **favorite** topping. I like strawberry, hot fudge, and **marshmallow** on mine! When you have the toppings **on** it is time to cover the whole **thing** with whipped cream. If you like nuts **you** can sprinkle some chopped peanuts or almonds **over** the whipped cream. Add a cherry to the top and you are done! Just one more thing... don't forget to eat it all!

bottom Cover cut favorite marshmallow need of on over the thing you

©1995 Kelley Wingate Publications, Inc.   61   KW 1014

Name _____   skill: cloze

Cloze

Cloze is a reading exercise where some of the words are missing and you must put them back in. Read the story below. Every eighth word has been taken out. Fill in the blanks with the words below the story.

Randy The Painter

Randy loved to paint. He liked to paint with his fingers **when** he was little. He would paint on **paper**. He would paint on tables. Once he **even** painted on the living room wall! Randy's **parents** were not happy with his painting. They **begged** him to play ball or ride his **bicycle**. But Randy only wanted to paint. When **Randy** was older he helped the neighbors paint **their** house. He painted a huge but beautiful **flower** on the front of their house. The **neighbors** did not want a huge beautiful flower **painted** on the front of their house. Randy **lost** that job! Today Randy is very happy. **He** is a famous painter. Now his parents **love** his painting. Now the neighbors wish they had the flower on the front of their house!

begged bicycle even flower He lost love neighbors painted paper parents Randy their when

©1995 Kelley Wingate Publications, Inc.   62   KW 1014

Name _____   skill: cloze

Cloze

Cloze is a reading exercise where some of the words are missing and you must put them back in. Read the story below. Every fifth word has been taken out. Fill in the blanks with the words below the story.

Nathan and the Cowboys

Nathan sat as still as he could on the shaky tree branch. No telling what might **happen** if those cowboys saw **him**. Three cowboys stood **below** the branch where Nathan **sat**. If they looked up **right** now they would see **him**. Nathan held his breath. **The** cowboys talked and laughed **for** a few minutes. They **moved** from the tree but **stopped** at the edge of **the** creek. The three braves **began** to splash each other **and** play in the water. **Nathan** relaxed a little. He **leaned** forward so he could **see** them through all the **leaves**. Suddenly Nathan lost his **balance** and fell. He hit **the** ground, rolling toward the **creek**. He looked up into the faces of the surprised cowboys!

and balance began below creek for happen him him leaned moved Nathan right sat see stopped The the the leaves

©1995 Kelley Wingate Publications, Inc.   63   KW 1014

Answer Key

Name _____   skill: point of view

Point of View

A story can be told from three points of view:
- **First person:** The main character tells the story using pronouns such as I, me, we, or us.
- **Limited third person:** A narrator tells the story as if he is watching it happen. Pronouns like he, she, it, they, and them are used.
- **Omniscient third person:** The narrator tells the story as if he is everywhere and knows everything, even what the characters are thinking and feeling.

Read each story and circle the point of view.

Charles stood on the sidewalk. He looked down the street. There was not a person in sight. He bent down and picked up the twenty dollar bill. He folded the bill carefully and put it in his pocket.

First Person   (Limited Third Person)   Omniscient Third Person

Charles stood on the sidewalk. His stomach was full of butterflies. Should he take the twenty dollar bill that was near his foot? No one was in sight. Charles knew someone would miss that money, but he really needed it. He bent down and picked up the bill. "I won't tell anyone I found it," he thought as he stuffed the money in his pocket.

First Person   Limited Third Person   (Omniscient Third Person)

I was standing on the sidewalk, thinking about what I could buy with that money. I looked, but did not see a single person on the street. I really needed that twenty dollars! No one needed to know that I found it. I felt uneasy taking the bill, but I quickly stuffed it into my pocket anyway.

(First Person)   Limited Third Person   Omniscient Third Person

©1995 Kelley Wingate Publications, Inc.   64   KW 1014

Name _____   skill: point of view

Point of View

A story can be told from three points of view:
- **First person:** The main character tells the story using pronouns such as I, me, we, or us.
- **Limited third person:** A narrator tells the story as if he is watching it happen. Pronouns like he, she, it, they, and them are used.
- **Omniscient third person:** The narrator tells the story as if he is everywhere and knows everything, even what the characters are thinking and feeling.

Read each story and circle the point of view.

I rode my bike up the steep hill. I was so hot and tired. It had been a long race, but I was in the lead! I raced down the other side of the hill. It began to rain a little. The cool wetness felt good on my face.

(First Person)   Limited Third Person   Omniscient Third Person

It was a hot day. The racers had gotten off to a good start. Susan quickly went ahead of the others. Her face was red and she began to sweat as she rode up the steep hill. It started to rain as she raced down the other side.

First Person   (Limited Third Person)   Omniscient Third Person

It was a hot day. The racers had gotten off to a good start. Susan quickly pulled ahead of the others. She was excited as she rode up the steep hill. Susan knew she was in the lead. She was hot and tired, but she barely cared. It began to rain as she raced down the other side of the hill. Susan felt cooler as the raindrops splashed her face.

First Person   Limited Third Person   (Omniscient Third Person)

©1995 Kelley Wingate Publications, Inc.   65   KW 1014

Name _____   skill: point of view

Point of View

Read each story and circle the point of view.

Buffy the squirrel sat on the fence. He eyed the blue jay carefully. Buffy wondered if he could get that big walnut away from such a big bird. The blue jay rolled the nut across the driveway, pecking at the hard shell. The bird really wanted that nut. Buffy licked his lips and thought about how good that nut was going to taste. He twitched his tail as he tried to decide what to do.

First Person   Limited Third Person   (Omniscient Third Person)

Buffy the squirrel sat on the fence. He was watching a blue jay on the driveway. The bird had a walnut and was trying to crack it open. The nut rolled across the cement. Buffy's tail twitched as if he was excited. He looked at the nut with eager eyes. He looked as if he was ready to pounce any second.

First Person   (Limited Third Person)   Omniscient Third Person

I watched that blue jay roll the walnut across the driveway. I could almost taste the nut in my mouth. Oh, would it make a tasty snack! The bird was pecking at the nut, trying to get it open. I wondered how I might steal that tasty tidbit without getting myself pecked by that sharp beak. I twitched my tail to help me think of a good plan. I really wanted that walnut!

(First Person)   Limited Third Person   Omniscient Third Person

©1995 Kelley Wingate Publications, Inc.   66   KW 1014

Name _____   skill: point of view

Point of View

A story can be told from three points of view:
- **First person:** The main character tells the story using pronouns such as I, me, we, or us.
- **Limited third person:** A narrator tells the story as if he is watching it happen. Pronouns like he, she, it, they, and them are used.
- **Omniscient third person:** The narrator tells the story as if he is everywhere and knows everything, even what the characters are thinking and feeling.

Read each story and circle the point of view.

Mark raced home as fast as he could. He dumped his books on the kitchen table and opened his notebook. He was barely seated before he began to work on his math problems. The teacher had given the class a huge amount of homework and Mark had the big game this afternoon. He had to finish his school work before he could go out to play. Mark glanced at the clock that was ticking loudly across the room. Only one hour to go. Could he finish in time?

First Person   (Limited Third Person)   Omniscient Third Person

I ran as fast as I could all the way home. Why did the teacher have to give us so much math homework tonight? I knew Mom would not let me go to the game if I didn't finish my school work first. The guys were counting on me to be at the game. I dumped my books on the kitchen table and got right to work. The ticking clock reminded me that I only had one hour to finish. Could I do it all in time?

(First Person)   Limited Third Person   Omniscient Third Person

Mark was anxious has he raced home. The teacher had given the class a huge math assignment for tomorrow. This afternoon was the most important ball game of the season. Mark knew his Mom would not let him go to the game if his work was not finished. Mark dumped his books on the kitchen table and got busy right away. He heard the loud ticking of the clock. He looked up and saw that he only had one hour to finish. His felt tense as he rushed through the problems, not caring if they were right or wrong. All Mark wanted to do was finish in time to go to the game. Could he do it?

First Person   Limited Third Person   (Omniscient Third Person)

©1995 Kelley Wingate Publications, Inc.   67   KW 1014

Answer Key

Name _____ skill: point of view

Point of View

Read each story and circle the point of view.

Penny and I had come to the library to work on our reports. I found several books and sat down to read them. Penny was looking for information she needed. Suddenly I felt a tapping on my shoulder. Penny put her finger to her lips and motioned for me to follow her. I knew right away that something was wrong. Her face looked white and she was scared. She pulled me behind a stack of books. "I saw that man come in here," she whispered. "The one we saw taking mail from Mrs. Smith's mailbox! Do you think he followed us?" We peeked around the bookshelf and, sure enough, there he was with his back to us.

(First Person)   Limited Third Person   Omniscient Third Person

Penny and Joan went to the library to work on their reports. Joan found several books and sat down to work. Penny was still looking for books when she saw a man come into the library. Her face turned white and her knees began to shake. Penny quietly tapped Joan's shoulder and motioned to her. The girls slipped behind a stack of books. Penny whispered, "I saw that man come in here. The one we saw taking mail from Mrs. Smith's mailbox! Do you think he followed us?" The girls peeked around the bookshelf and saw the man standing with his back to them.

First Person   (Limited Third Person)   Omniscient Third Person

Penny and Joan went to the library to work on their reports. Joan found several books and sat down to work. Penny was still looking for her books when she saw a man come into the library. Penny's heart skipped a beat as she recognized him. She knew she had to get to Joan before the man saw them. Penny tapped Joan's shoulder and pulled her behind a stack of books. She whispered, "I saw that man come in here. The one we saw taking mail from Mrs. Smith's mailbox! Do you think he followed us?" Joan felt weak in the knees when she saw the man standing with his back to them.

First Person   Limited Third person   (Omniscient Third Person)

©1995 Kelley Wingate Publications, Inc.   68   KW 1014

Name _____ skill: compare and contrast

Compare and Contrast

Compare the words in each row below. Circle the two words that go together then write a sentence telling how they are alike.

1. (marsh) (lagoon) plant
   Both places with water
2. (shimmer) dull (glow)
   Both shine
3. (lawyer) (clerk) bride
   Both work with the law
4. (foggy) temperature (sunny)
   Both are types of weather
5. pioneer (reindeer) (hamster)
   Both are animals
6. (vast) tiny (enormous)
   Both mean big
7. (Halloween) (Christmas) Europe
   Both are holidays

Think Ahead: Can you find a group that fits all three words in each row?

©1995 Kelley Wingate Publications, Inc.   69   KW 1014

Name _____ skill: compare and contrast

Compare and Contrast

Compare the words in each row below. Circle the two words that go together then write a sentence telling how they are alike.

1. (karate) (soccer) ball
   Both are sports
2. (roost) (nest) shed
   Both are where an animal lives.
3. (piano) radio (tuba)
   Both are musical instruments.
4. huge (thousand) (million)
   Both are numbers
5. (scare) eerie (happy)
   Both are emotions
6. baseball (hitter) (batter)
   Both are people
7. (beetle) beast (gnat)
   Both are insects

Think Ahead: Can you find a group that fits all three words in each row?

©1995 Kelley Wingate Publications, Inc.   70   KW 1014

Name _____ skill: compare and contrast

Compare and Contrast

Compare the words in each row below. Circle the two words that go together then write a sentence telling how they are alike.

1. (harsh) mellow (stern)
   Both are severe
2. bed (stool) (chair)
   We can sit on both
3. (stroll) (walk) race
   Both are slow
4. (savage) tame (wild)
   Both have no control
5. (tune) (melody) piano
   Both are music
6. tree (limb) (branch)
   Both are on a tree
7. (active) resting (busy)
   Both are movement
8. (grim) funny (serious)
   Both are sombre

Think Ahead: Can you find a group that fits all three words in each row?

©1995 Kelley Wingate Publications, Inc.   71   KW 1014

Answer Key

Name _____ skill: compare and contrast

Compare and Contrast

Compare the words in each row below. Circle the two words that go together then write a sentence telling how they are alike.

1. (grey) (tan) stripe

Both are colors

2. (canoe) (steamship) railroad

Both travel in water

3. dollar (nickel) (dime)

Both are coins

4. (hornet) (wasp) butterfly

Both insects can sting

5. (hurricane) breeze (earthquake)

Both are natural diasters

6. (icicle) (frozen) sled

Both are frozen water

Think Ahead: Can you find a group that fits all three words in each row ?

©1995 Kelley Wingate Publications, Inc.   72   KW 1014

Name _____ skill: compare and contrast

Compare and Contrast

Compare the words in each row below. Circle the two words that go together then write a sentence telling how they are alike.

1. (macaroni) (spaghetti) soup

Both are a type of pasta

2. fish (lobster) (crab)

Both are crustacians

3. (blossom) (flower) leaf

Both make seeds

4. (sink) kitchen (oven)

Both are work areas in a kitchen

5. (stone) (boulder) dirt

Both are types of rocks

6. beneath (northwest) (south)

Both are directions

7. (praise) (flatter) insult

Both are compliments

8. (midnight) month (noon)

Both are times of day

Think Ahead: Can you find a group that fits all three words in each row ?

©1995 Kelley Wingate Publications, Inc.   73   KW 1014

Name _____ skill: prefixes

Prefix "un"

The prefix **un** means "not". Make prefixes out of these words by adding **un** before each word. Use the new words in the sentences below.

lucky — unlucky
roll — unroll
able — unable
certain — uncertain
kind — unkind
cover — uncover
easy — uneasy
friendly — unfriendly

1. Ken was _uncertain_ about which path to take back to camp.
2. I was so _unlucky_ I couldn't even win at simple games.
3. Kevin was _unkind_ to Sue when he laughed at her mistake.
4. Jack was so _unfriendly_ he wouldn't even talk to us.
5. Please _uncover_ that box so I can put these blocks in it.
6. The wrapping paper will _unroll_ easily if you pull it just right.
7. Susan felt _uneasy_ when the teacher looked at her math test.
8. Kelly is _unable_ to play outside right now.

©1995 Kelley Wingate Publications, Inc.   74   KW 1014

Name _____ skill: prefixes

Prefix: "un"

The prefix **un** means "not". Make prefixes out of these words by adding **un** before each word. Use the new words in the sentences below.

made — unmade
grateful — ungrateful
equal — unequal
happy — unhappy
lit — unlit
helpful — unhelpful
hook — unhook
necessary — unnecessary

1. The class was _unhappy_ when the teacher gave them extra homework.
2. A history book is _unhelpful_ when I am looking for answers to science questions.
3. It was _unnecessary_ to drive all the way to the bank because I had money in my pocket.
4. The spoiled child was _ungrateful_ for all his new gifts.
5. An _unlit_ room is very dark at midnight.
6. Can you _unhook_ those drapes for me, please?
7. Our pieces of cake are _unequal_. Yours is larger than mine!
8. We left the beds _unmade_ this morning because we were in a hurry.

©1995 Kelley Wingate Publications, Inc.   75   KW 1014

Answer Key

Page 76

Name _____   skill: prefixes

Prefix: "Re"

The prefix **re** means "again". Make prefixes out of these words by adding **re** before each word. Use the new words in the sentences below.

do	**redo**
call	**recall**
write	**rewrite**
mark	**remark**
paint	**repaint**
live	**relive**
move	**remove**
name	**rename**

1. Joey must **redo** his math problems because they are all wrong.
2. Mary will use soap and water to **remove** the stain from her blouse.
3. I thought I heard you make a **remark** about my new boots. Did you say you liked them?
4. The old paint is peeling off the house. We will have to **repaint** it soon.
5. I have to **rewrite** this paper because there are too many words spelled wrong.
6. Can you **relive** what you did on your last birthday?
7. We will **rename** our clubhouse because we don't like the name "Tigers" anymore.
8. I do not like to **recall** memories that are painful to me.

©1995 Kelley Wingate Publications, Inc.   76   KW 1014

Page 77

Name _____   skill: prefixes

Prefix: "Re"

The prefix **re** means "again". Make prefixes out of these words by adding **re** before each word. Use the new words in the sentences below.

mind	**remind**
place	**replace**
wind	**rewind**
word	**reword**
make	**remake**
turn	**return**
wash	**rewash**
heat	**reheat**

1. You will have to **remake** the bed because you did not do a good job the first time.
2. Mom said we have to **rewind** this video tape before we can play another one.
3. Do not break this glass because it is very old and I cannot **replace** it.
4. I do not like the way my paper sounds. Can you help me **reword** it?
5. The wind blew the clean sheets off the clothesline. Now we have to **rewash** all of them.
6. Please **reheat** my soup because it has become cold.
7. It is time to **return** these library books!
8. Can you **remind** me that I have to leave at four o'clock? I tend to forget sometimes.

©1995 Kelley Wingate Publications, Inc.   77   KW 1014

Page 78

Name _____   skill: prefixes

Prefix: "Under"

The prefix **under** means "below". Make prefixes out of these words by adding **under** before each word. Use the new words in the sentences below.

foot	**underfoot**
cover	**undercover**
water	**underwater**
ground	**underground**
wear	**underwear**
done	**underdone**
ripe	**underipe**
weight	**underweight**

1. The doctor said Jimmy is a little **underweight**. He needs to put on ten pounds by next month.
2. It rained so hard our street was **underwater** and we couldn't go anywhere.
3. That pineapple is **underripe** and not ready to eat yet.
4. The policeman had to go **undercover** to catch the thief.
5. A subway is a train that travels **underground**.
6. Our new puppy was **underfoot**, causing us to trip all the time.
7. My aunt always gives me new **underwear** for my birthday.
8. The meat was **underdone** and we had to cook it more before we could eat it.

©1995 Kelley Wingate Publications, Inc.   78   KW 1014

Page 79

Name _____   skill: prefixes

Prefix: "After"

The prefix **after** means "after or later". Make prefixes out of these words by adding **after** before each word. Use the new words in the sentences below.

noon	**afternoon**
taste	**aftertaste**
thought	**afterthought**
life	**afterlife**
ward	**afterward**
care	**aftercare**
glow	**afterglow**
time	**aftertime**

1. The school has **aftercare** so children can stay until dinner time.
2. The flash from the camera had an **afterglow**, lighting the room for a few seconds.
3. We are going on a picnic this **afternoon**.
4. The onions left a strong **aftertaste** in my mouth.
5. Many people believe that there is an **afterlife** when we die.
6. Steve had an **afterthought** when he had finished speaking. He wrote it down so he wouldn't forget it.
7. We will go to the movie now and get a hamburger **afterward**.
8. The **aftertime** is the future!

©1995 Kelley Wingate Publications, Inc.   79   KW 1014

©1995 Kelley Wingate Publications, Inc.   126   CD-3711

Answer Key

Name _____   skill: prefixes

Prefix: "Mis"

The prefix **mis** means "bad". Make prefixes out of these words by adding **mis** before each word. Use the new words in the sentences below.

behaving	misbehaving
fortune	misfortune
take	mistake
lead	mislead
laid	mislaid
adventure	misadventure
matched	mismatched
read	misread

1. I am afraid I have **mislaid** the keys again. I cannot find them anywhere.
2. After our last **misadventure** I am afraid to try skiing again.
3. David made only one **mistake** on his spelling test!
4. The children were **misbehaving** and were sent to the principal's office.
5. Yesterday I had the **misfortune** of breaking my leg.
6. Kevin had on a **mismatched** pair of socks. One was black and the other was brown!
7. Sally **misread** the sign. She thought it said "field" instead of "yield".
8. I did not mean to **mislead** you about the play. I said you had a part in it, but I did not say you were the star!

©1995 Kelley Wingate Publications, Inc.   80   KW 1014

Name _____   skill: prefixes

Prefix: "Out"

The prefix **out** means "beyond". Make prefixes out of these words by adding **out** before each word. Use the new words in the sentences below.

last	outlast
run	outrun
do	outdo
live	outlive
number	outnumber
rage	outrage
look	outlook
grow	outgrow

1. Daniel is getting such big feet he will soon **outgrow** those shoes!
2. Tina always has a happy **outlook** on life. She thinks everything that happens is good.
3. Our cat is much younger than our dog. The cat will probably **outlive** the dog by a few years.
4. I cannot **outdo** your science project because it is the best one I have ever seen!
5. There are seven boys and only three girls at the party. The boys **outnumber** the girls.
6. I am drinking my soda slowly. My drink will **outlast** yours because you are gulping your soda quickly.
7. I'll bet I can **outrun** you in a foot race!
8. Beth flew into an **outrage** when she learned she did not win the contest.

©1995 Kelley Wingate Publications, Inc.   81   KW 1014

Name _____   skill: prefixes

Prefix: "Over"

The prefix **over** means "too much". Make prefixes out of these words by adding **over** before each word. Use the new words in the sentences below.

heat	overheat
stuffed	overstuffed
price	overprice
looks	overlooks
board	overboard
acts	overacts
dressed	overdressed
fill	overfill

1. Bill never gets a part in the play because he **overacts** at tryouts.
2. My uncle fell **overboard** when we went sailing last week.
3. Do not **overprice** your cookies or no one will want to buy them.
4. Do not **overfill** the gas tank or it will spill on the ground.
5. Kathy wore a velvet dress to the pool party. She was very **overdressed**
6. Our bedroom window **overlooks** a beautiful park below.
7. If you **overheat** the soup it will burn your mouth!
8. I ate too much dinner and now I am **overstuffed**!

©1995 Kelley Wingate Publications, Inc.   82   KW 1014

Name _____   skill: prefixes

Prefix: "Be"

The prefix **be** means "make". Make prefixes out of these words by adding **be** before each word. Use the new words in the sentences below.

side	beside
friend	befriend
cause	because
come	become
witch	bewitch
hind	behind
ware	beware
low	below

1. Vicky put the forks **beside** the plates as she set the table.
2. Hang your hat on the hook just **below** mine.
3. It is important to **beware** when you are walking alone at night.
4. Watch out! It is said that a cat can **bewitch** you on Halloween night.
5. I will **become** a better speller when I learn to check my work.
6. Connie would like to **befriend** the new girl because she seems so lonely.
7. Do not stand **behind** the door or you may get hit when someone opens it.
8. John must go to bed early tonight **because** he is going fishing early tomorrow morning.

©1995 Kelley Wingate Publications, Inc.   83   KW 1014

Answer Key

Name _____   skill: contractions

Contractions

Read the sentences below. Circle the correct contraction for the underlined words.

1. I am going to the zoo tomorrow.
   I'd   I'll   (I'm)

2. You are my best friend!
   you'd   you'll   (you're)

3. Are you sure we are on the right path?
   we'd   we'll   (we're)

4. Brian said he is older than you.
   he'd   (he's)   he'll

5. I think these will make fine curtains for the clubhouse.
   there's   (these'll)   they'll

6. I did not look at the movie when it was scary!
   (didn't)   did'nt   don't

7. Who would want to live in that dusty old house?
   (who'd)   who's   who've

8. We might not need to cut the grass this week.
   might've   (mightn't)   mayn't

9. I do not have the right book, but this will do just fine.
   it'll   that'll   (this'll)

10. They are very kind people.
   They'll   (They're)   They've

©1995 Kelley Wingate Publications, Inc.   84   KW 1014

Name _____   skill: contractions

Contractions

Read the sentences below. Circle the correct contraction for the underlined words.

1. Lucy does not like to swim in the lake.
   don't   didn't   (doesn't)

2. Mother said that she would take us to the park today.
   she'll   (she'd)   she's

3. Who are those new people that just moved here?
   Who'll   (Who're)   Who's

4. We have not had time to unpack our suitcases yet.
   hadn't   hasn't   (haven't)

5. Do you think we could have missed the right turn?
   can't   couldn't   (could've)

6. Do you think you will want a snack before bedtime?
   (you'll)   you're   you've

7. We are not really sure who the sweater belongs to.
   are'nt   (aren't)   isn't

8. Mrs. Jones was certain that there would be enough food for all our guests.
   there'll   (there'd)   there's

9. Who is going to the lake with us?
   Who'll   (Who's)   Won't

10. Judy said that they will be a little late getting here.
   they'd   (they'll)   they've

©1995 Kelley Wingate Publications, Inc.   85   KW 1014

Name _____   skill: contractions

Contractions

Read the sentences below. Circle the correct contraction for the underlined words.

1. Let us move on to the next room of the museum now.
   Lets   (Let's)   Let'us

2. We should have known that Carol would be late. She always is!
   shouldn't   should't   (should've)

3. The books were not on the shelves where they belonged.
   wasn't   (weren't)   where'd

4. You have to do your homework before you can go out to play.
   You'll   You're   (You've)

5. Patty promised that will be the best cake she has ever baked.
   that'd   (that'll)   that's

6. Amy said she would love to go to the show with Mike.
   (she'd)   she'll   she's

7. That is my favorite pair of pants.
   That'd   That'll   (That's)

8. I told you I would not have any candy left by the end of the day!
   won't   (wouldn't)   would've

9. I have at least six more pages to write before I will be done.
   I'd   I'm   (I've)

10. I will not use any of your paper if you would rather I did not.
   wasn't   willn't   (won't)

©1995 Kelley Wingate Publications, Inc.   86   KW 1014

Name _____   skill: contractions

Contractions

Read the sentences below. Circle the correct contraction for the underlined words.

1. What will you bring to the party?
   What'd   (What'll)   What's

2. Mark and Tracy said they have been waiting for over an hour to get tickets.
   they'll   they're   (they've)

3. Those will be the biggest pancakes we have ever made!
   That'll   (Those'll)   These'll

4. Who will go shopping with me?
   Who'd   (Who'll)   Who's

5. John said he will be happy to fix the car for us.
   (he'll)   he'd   he's

6. They are a great group of children!
   They'd   (They're)   They'll

7. I could not see over the fence so I looked through the gate.
   can't   could'nt   (couldn't)

8. Billy enjoys eating donuts. He thinks they are very sweet tasting.
   they'll   (they're)   they've

9. Karen knows she should not be angry with her sister.
   (shouldn't)   should've   can't

10. Nancy had not noticed the sign for the wet paint.
   (hadn't)   had'nt   hasn't

©1995 Kelley Wingate Publications, Inc.   87   KW 1014

Answer Key

Contractions

Contractions

Read the sentences below. Circle the correct contraction for the underlined words.

1. <u>What would</u> you think if you saw a pink elephant?
   What's (What'd) What'll

2. Martha thinks <u>she is</u> the smartest girl in school.
   she'd she'll (she's)

3. <u>We will</u> be the first ones at the party if we leave now.
   We'd (We'll) We're

4. <u>There have</u> been six flights into space this past month.
   There'd They've (There've)

5. I can see that <u>it is</u> getting pretty late.
   (It's) It'll I've

6. The <u>door was not</u> locked all night.
   (wasn't) won't wouldn't

7. You <u>need not</u> have bothered getting the guest room ready because we are <u>not</u> staying.
   (needn't) didn't should've

8. <u>Who will</u> go first?
   (Who'll) Who're Who's

9. Bobby said he <u>can not</u> come to my house after school today.
   (can't) couldn't could've

10. <u>There will</u> be a short rest time after we finish walking this mile.
    (There'll) There's There've

©1995 Kelley Wingate Publications, Inc.   88   KW 1014

Suffixes (page 89)

Suffixes

Words are changed when you add a suffix to them. Put the right word in each sentence.

excite excitement
1. Watching a good movie can __excite__ me. The __excitement__ makes me happy.

add addition
2. The new room is an __addition__ to our house. We had to __add__ the room because we needed more space.

sell seller
3. Joe likes to __sell__ cars. He is a __seller__ for the Used Car Company.

active activity
4. Mrs. Kline likes to stay __active__ and do many things. She says the __activity__ makes her feel healthy.

light lighten
5. Dad put a new __light__ in my bedroom. He said the room was a little dark and we needed to __lighten__ it.

spoon spoonful
6. I need a __spoon__ to mix the cookie dough. Please add a __spoonful__ of water because it is too dry.

depart departing
7. The airplane will be __departing__ in one hour. It is time for us to __depart__ for the airport.

brave bravery
8. Roger is a very __brave__ boy. He even got a medal for his __bravery__.

©1995 Kelley Wingate Publications, Inc.   89   KW 1014

Suffixes (page 90)

Suffixes

Words are changed when you add a suffix to them. Put the right word in each sentence.

amuse amusement
1. Bob loves to __amuse__ his friends by acting like a clown. His friends like the __amusement__ of watching him.

wisp wispy
2. Lauren pushed a __wisp__ of hair out of her face. She needed a haircut because her hair was too __wispy__ around her face.

speak speaker
3. I was asked to be the main __speaker__ to make the presentation for my club. I will have to __speak__ in front of a lot of people!

respect respectful
4. My mother says I must be __respectful__ of older people. It is important to show my __respect__.

explore exploration
5. Jim loves to __explore__ caves. He thinks that cave __exploration__ is more fun than anything.

pain painful
6. I have a __painful__ sore on the bottom of my foot. Every step I take causes me more __pain__.

tingle tingled
7. Her fingers __tingled__ as she felt the electricity run through them. Even the top of her arms began to __tingle__.

value valuable
8. This old coin is very __valuable__. I don't know the exact __value__, but I do know it is worth a lot of money.

©1995 Kelley Wingate Publications, Inc.   90   KW 1014

Suffixes (page 91)

Suffixes

Words are changed when you add a suffix to them. Put the right word in each sentence.

decorate decorations
1. It is fun to __decorate__ the classroom for a holiday. My favorite __decorations__ are the balloons that float to the ceiling.

perform performance
2. Erin will __perform__ on stage next week. She is practicing so her __performance__ will be the best she can do.

thrill thrilling
3. I find it __thrilling__ to sit in the front row at the movies. When the movie gets scary it is a real __thrill__ to me!

fear fearless
4. My brother has no __fear__ of dark rooms. He is __fearless__ and can walk right in without turning on the light.

begin beginner
5. I will __begin__ to take piano lessons next week. I am in the __beginner__ class.

select selection
6. Kim must __select__ a gift for her best friend. She will make her __selection__ at the gift shop in town.

easy easily
7. Simon __easily__ won the spelling contest. Spelling is a subject that is very __easy__ for him.

argue argument
8. I __argue__ a lot with my brother. Just this morning we had an __arguement__ over whose turn it was to clean our room.

©1995 Kelley Wingate Publications, Inc.   91   KW 1014

Answer Key

Suffixes

Words are changed when you add a suffix to them. Put the right word in each sentence.

1. Jan loves to _____**create**_____ **create creation** animals with her clay. Her latest _____**creations**_____ was a creature with three legs and four eyes.

2. Mother was _____**stitching**_____ **stitch stitching** my old playclothes when I came rushing in the room. She took the last _____**stitch**_____ before she asked me what I wanted.

3. Tony was going to _____**exhibit**_____ **exhibit exhibited** his black rabbit at the fair this year. Last year Tony took first place when he _____**exhibited**_____ his white rabbit.

4. Mr. Potts is a great _____**gardener**_____ **garden gardener**. His _____**garden**_____ is the best one in town.

5. I believe I will _____**invent**_____ **invent inventor** something important one day. My dream is to be a famous _____**inventor**_____.

6. The bakery always has an _____**advertisement**_____ **advertise advertisement** in the window. They like to _____**advertise**_____ because it makes people come in to shop there.

7. Today feels like a _____**lazy**_____ **lazy lazily** day. I stayed in bed and _____**lazily**_____ watched as the sun climbed high in the sky.

Suffixes

Words are changed when you add a suffix to them. Put the right word in each sentence.

1. Jill has _____**numerous**_____ **number numerous** pencils in her pencil box. There are so many I can't count to the _____**number**_____ she has!

2. My mother is my favorite _____**relation**_____ **relation relationship**. We have a very close _____**relationship**_____.

3. I watched in _____**astonishment**_____ **astonish astonishment** as the magician did the trick with fire. It takes a lot to _____**astonish**_____ me, but he was really good!

4. The judge said _____**congratulations**_____ **congratulate congratulations** to Jimmy, the winner of the science fair. I went over to _____**congratulate**_____ him, too.

5. There was a box for _____**suggestions**_____ **suggest suggestions** by the door. I knew what I wanted to _____**suggest**_____ so I wrote it down and put it in the box.

6. I don't think this story is very _____**believable**_____ **believe believable**. I do not _____**believe**_____ in monsters or witches anymore.

7. Alice tried to _____**warn**_____ **warn warning** the boaters that a storm was quickly moving in. Her _____**warning**_____ came too late. The boaters were caught in the raging storm.

8. Sharon hung her clothes _____**neatly**_____ **neat neatly** on their hangers. She liked to keep her room _____**neat**_____ and tidy.

Multiple Meanings

Many words have more than one meaning. Sometimes you can figure out which meaning is correct by seeing how the word was used in a sentence. If you cannot figure it out, look the word up in the dictionary.

In each sentence below a word has been underlined. There are two definitions given for the underlined word. Decide which meaning is correct by reading the sentence and thinking about how the word was used. Write the correct meaning on the line.

1. The bail was broken so the bucket full of water was difficult to lift.
   a. throw water out   b. handle of a pail
   _____**handle of a pail**_____

2. The princess had a grand time at the ball last night.
   a. a dance   b. a round object
   _____**a dance**_____

3. The rabbit hide will make a warm pair of mittens.
   a. to keep out of sight   b. an animal skin
   _____**an animal skin**_____

4. Joe left before I could tell him goodbye.
   a. the opposite of right   b. went away
   _____**went away**_____

5. Jack had a fit when his brother broke his new bicycle.
   a. suitable   b. sudden attack
   _____**sudden attack**_____

6. The group became grave when they saw the danger they were in.
   a. serious   b. a place of burial
   _____**serious**_____

7. The mortar between the bricks was beginning to crumble.
   a. a cement mixture   b. a short cannon
   _____**a cement mixture**_____

8. The crash was so hard it jarred my body!
   a. a container   b. rattled
   _____**rattled**_____

Multiple Meanings

Many words have more than one meaning. Sometimes you can figure out which meaning is correct by seeing how the word was used in a sentence. If you cannot figure it out, look the word up in the dictionary.

In each sentence below a word has been underlined. There are two definitions given for the underlined word. Decide which meaning is correct by reading the sentence and thinking about how the word was used. Write the correct meaning on the line.

1. The boy was lean because he ate healthy foods and exercised.
   a. slanting   b. not fat
   _____**not fat**_____

2. The farmer built a new pen to keep the pigs in.
   a. writing tool   b. enclosed yard
   _____**enclosed yard**_____

3. Kathy was dizzy so she held on to the chair to stable herself.
   a. building for horses   b. steady
   _____**steady**_____

4. That Nancy can sure yak! She kept me on the phone for two hours!
   a. talk endlessly   b. a long-haired ox
   _____**talk endlessly**_____

5. Go to the kitchen tap and fill this bottle with water.
   a. strike lightly   b. faucet
   _____**faucet**_____

6. This table is built so well, it should last forever.
   a. at the end   b. continue
   _____**continue**_____

7. Sam needs a smaller bit for this hole. The one he has is too big for the screw.
   a. did bite   b. tool for drilling
   _____**tool for drilling**_____

8. The puppy will cock his head when he is puzzled.
   a. tilt upward   b. rooster
   _____**tilt upward**_____

Answer Key

Name _____ skill: multiple meanings

Multiple Meanings

Many words have more than one meaning. Sometimes you can figure out which meaning is correct by seeing how the word was used in a sentence. If you cannot figure it out, look the word up in the dictionary.

In each sentence below a word has been underlined. There are two definitions given for the underlined word. Decide which meaning is correct by reading the sentence and thinking about how the word was used. Write the correct meaning on the line.

1. I do not mean to carp, but I am tired of telling you to clean your room.
   a. complain   b. kind of fish
   Complain

2. Justin wants to mine for diamonds on his land.
   a. belonging to me   b. hole in the earth
   hole in the earth

3. Please draw a ring around the correct answer.
   a. circle   b. bell sound
   circle

4. Do you have a present for Mary's birthday party?
   a. not absent   b. gift
   gift

5. Steep the tea bag for three minutes if you want strong tea.
   a. having a sharp slope   b. soak
   soak

6. The swimmer was almost drowned when the wake covered her head.
   a. stop sleeping   b. trail left behind a ship
   trail left behind a ship

7. This was a job well done!
   a. satisfactory   b. hole dug for water
   satisfactory

8. The nurse will tend to your cut now.
   a. take care of   b. incline to
   take care of

©1995 Kelley Wingate Publications, Inc.   96   KW 1014

Multiple Meanings

Many words have more than one meaning. Sometimes you can figure out which meaning is correct by seeing how the word was used in a sentence. If you cannot figure it out, look the word up in the dictionary.

In each sentence below a word has been underlined. There are two definitions given for the underlined word. Decide which meaning is correct by reading the sentence and thinking about how the word was used. Write the correct meaning on the line.

1. Did you see Jim vault that fence without even touching it?
   a. a safe for valuables   b. jump over
   jump over

2. Put the string on this reel so we can use it next time.
   a. spool for winding   b. lively dance
   spool for winding

3. Abbey and I played three games of pool this weekend.
   a. tank with water   b. a game with balls on a table
   a game with balls on a table

4. The angry driver began to rail at the bus driver who ran into his car.
   a. bar of wood or metal   b. complain bitterly
   complain bitterly

5. This movie is very much like the book I just read.
   a. similar to   b. be pleased with
   similar to

6. John is the elder of the two boys.
   a. older   b. small tree
   older

7. The chef poured the batter into a large baking pan.
   a. liquid   b. baseball player
   liquid

8. We can alight from the airplane now.
   a. get down from   b. on fire
   get down from

©1995 Kelley Wingate Publications, Inc.   97   KW 1014

Multiple Meanings

Many words have more than one meaning. Sometimes you can figure out which meaning is correct by seeing how the word was used in a sentence. If you cannot figure it out, look the word up in the dictionary.

In each sentence below a word has been underlined. There are two definitions given for the underlined word. Decide which meaning is correct by reading the sentence and thinking about how the word was used. Write the correct meaning on the line.

1. The boys blazed a path through the thick underbrush.
   a. fire   b. marked a trail
   marked a trail

2. Dad cooked the chop a little too much and it tasted dry.
   a. cut with something sharp   b. cut of meat
   cut of meat

3. Clip on the papers so they stay together.
   a. cut   b. fasten
   fasten

4. The present was in a large box wrapped in brown paper.
   a. four sided container   b. to fight with fists
   four sided container

5. My jeans are beginning to fray a little at the bottom.
   a. become ragged   b. fight
   become ragged

6. The sailor closed the hatch so the water could not get in his room.
   a. come out of an egg   b. an opening in the deck
   an opening in the deck

7. The nap of the carpet is wearing down.
   a. short sleep   b. rug fuzz
   rug fuzz

8. The mole dug tunnels all over our front lawn.
   a. brown spot on the skin   b. small underground animal
   small underground animal

©1995 Kelley Wingate Publications, Inc.   98   KW 1014

Multiple Meanings

Many words have more than one meaning. Sometimes you can figure out which meaning is correct by seeing how the word was used in a sentence. If you cannot figure it out, look the word up in the dictionary.

In each sentence below a word has been underlined. There are two definitions given for the underlined word. Decide which meaning is correct by reading the sentence and thinking about how the word was used. Write the correct meaning on the line.

1. Joel burned his palm on the hot stove.
   a. inside of the hand   b. kind of tree
   inside of the hand

2. Kelly cut a spray from the rose bush.
   a. sprinkle liquid   b. small branch with leaves and flowers
   small branch with leaves and flowers

3. I found a slug in the garden.
   a. small slow-moving animal   b. to hit hard
   small slow-moving animal

4. The toll on the bridge was one dollar.
   a. sound of a bell   b. fee paid to use something
   fee paid to use something

5. Grandma liked to sit on the front stoop and watch the neighborhood.
   a. bend down   b. porch
   porch

6. Greg will take six of the pencils and you can have the rest.
   a. sleep   b. what is left
   what is left

7. Please get the clippers and prune that bush.
   a. fruit   b. trim
   trim

8. Mrs. Smith has six boys to rear.
   a. the back part   b. bring up
   bring up

©1995 Kelley Wingate Publications, Inc.   99   KW 1014

Answer Key

Multiple Meanings

Many words have more than one meaning. Sometimes you can figure out which meaning is correct by seeing how the word was used in a sentence. If you cannot figure it out, look the word up in the dictionary.

In each sentence below a word has been underlined. There are two definitions given for the underlined word. Decide which meaning is correct by reading the sentence and thinking about how the word was used. Write the correct meaning on the line.

1. The husky was strong enough to pull the sled by himself!
   a. big and strong   b. a kind of dog
   a kind of dog
2. Karen was so weak her legs and arms were limp.
   a. lame walk   b. not stiff
   not stiff
3. Jane wore a jumper to school today.
   a. person or thing that jumps   b. type of dress
   type of dress
4. If I can get their map I might be able to foil their plans for the robbery.
   a. prevent or stop   b. metal wrapping
   prevent or stop
5. The balloon was grazing the ceiling.
   a. feed on grass   b. gently touching
   gently touching
6. It is not healthy to fast for more than a day or two.
   a. go without food   b. speedy
   go without food
7. A crow made a nest in the old pine tree.
   a. loud cry of a rooster   b. large black bird
   large black bird
8. Poor Donna has a case of the measles!
   a. condition   b. box or container
   condition

Multiple Meanings

Many words have more than one meaning. Sometimes you can figure out which meaning is correct by seeing how the word was used in a sentence. If you cannot figure it out, look the word up in the dictionary.

In each sentence below a word has been underlined. There are two definitions given for the underlined word. Decide which meaning is correct by reading the sentence and thinking about how the word was used. Write the correct meaning on the line.

1. I do not like long speeches because they bore me.
   a. make a hole   (b.) make weary
2. Sammy can bowl very well at Park Ten Lanes.
   a. rounded dish   (b.) play a game with pins and a ball
3. The cold winter weather can chap your hands quickly.
   (a.) crack or roughen   b. boy or man
4. The woman did not bat an eyelash at the high price she was charged.
   a. flying mammal   (b.) wink
5. We put a band around the cards to keep them together.
   a. group of musicians   (b.) thin strip that binds
6. The bank was slippery and muddy so we walked in the water.
   a. a place of business   (b.) land along a river
7. The man had a bass voice that sounded warm and nice.
   (a.) low sound   b. kind of fish
8. The boat began to bob as the waves grew bigger.
   a. nickname for Robert   (b.) move up and down

Multiple Meanings

Many words have more than one meaning. Sometimes you can figure out which meaning is correct by seeing how the word was used in a sentence. If you cannot figure it out, look the word up in the dictionary.

In each sentence below a word has been underlined. There are two definitions given for the underlined word. Decide which meaning is correct by reading the sentence and thinking about how the word was used. Write the correct meaning on the line.

1. The coyote will bay at a full moon.
   a. part of a sea   b. howl
   howl
2. The town began to boom as more people moved there.
   a. sudden increase in size   b. deep sound
   sudden increase in size
3. I am bound to become a movie star some day!
   a. on the way   b. spring back
   on the way
4. Who made this delicious blueberry cobbler?
   a. one who mends shoes   b. fruit pie with one crust
   fruit pie with one crust
5. Mark took a walk around the compound before turning in for the night.
   a. having more than one part   b. enclosed yard
   enclosed yard
6. Take a count to see if everyone is here.
   a. name numbers in order   b. a nobleman
   name numbers in order
7. The pies were sitting on the counter in the kitchen.
   a. long table top   b. one who counts
   long table top
8. What is the date for the fair this year?
   a. day, month, and year   b. sweet dark fruit
   day, month, and year

Multiple Meanings

Many words have more than one meaning. Sometimes you can figure out which meaning is correct by seeing how the word was used in a sentence. If you cannot figure it out, look the word up in the dictionary.

In each sentence below a word has been underlined. There are two definitions given for the underlined word. Decide which meaning is correct by reading the sentence and thinking about how the word was used. Write the correct meaning on the line.

1. My boss said he would dock my pay if I am late once more.
   a. wharf   b. cut some off
   cut some off
2. The best pillows are made of down.
   a. soft feathers   b. grassy land
   soft feathers
3. I must say that Brad is a sharp dresser.
   a. one who dresses   b. chest of drawers
   one who dresses
4. We rented a flat with two bedrooms.
   a. smooth   b. apartment
   apartment
5. The deer was fleet so we didn't see her for long.
   a. group of ships   b. quick
   quick
6. It is time to file some of these papers!
   a. to put in order in a drawer   b. to smooth the rough edges
   to put in order in a drawer
7. Meghan tripped over a rock and began to flounder in the shallow water.
   a. struggle   b. kind of fish
   struggle
8. Hail a cab so we won't have to walk in the rain.
   a. pieces of ice that fall like rain   b. shout or call out to
   shout or call out to

Answer Key

Name _____   skill: analogies

Analogies

Analogies compare relationships of words. For example:

chair is to sit as bed is to _____

The relationship of chair and sit (you sit in a chair) is compared to the relationship between bed and what you do in it (you sleep in a bed). The missing word is bed.

Find the missing word in these analogies.

in is to out as up is to ___down___
two is to four as three is to ___six___
snow is to cold as sun is to ___hot___
mother is to aunt as father is to ___uncle___
ear is to hear as eye is to ___see___
she is to her as he is to ___him___
dog is to bark as bird is to ___chirp___
brother is to boy as sister is to ___girl___
bear is to den as bee is to ___hive___
finger is to hand as toe is to ___foot___
girl is to mother as boy is to ___father___
left is to right as top is to ___bottom___

©1995 Kelley Wingate Publications, Inc.   104   KW 1014

Name _____   skill: analogies

Analogies 2

Analogies compare relationships of words. For example:

chair is to sit as bed is to _____

The relationship of chair and sit (you sit in a chair) is compared to the relationship between bed and what you do in it (you sleep in a bed). The missing word is bed.

Find the missing word in these analogies.

car is to driver as plane is to ___pilot___
bird is to sky as fish is to ___water___
coffee is to drink as hamburger is to ___eat___
small is to tiny as large is to ___big___
glove is to hand as boot is to ___foot___
easy is to simple as hard is to ___difficult___
breakfast is to lunch as morning is to ___afternoon___
blue is to color as round is to ___shape___
date is to calendar as time is to ___clock___
win is to lose as stop is to ___go___
minute is to hour as day is to ___week___
paw is to dog as fin is to ___fish___

©1995 Kelley Wingate Publications, Inc.   105   KW 1014

Name _____   skill: analogies

Analogies 3

Analogies compare relationships of words. For example:

chair is to sit as bed is to _____

The relationship of chair and sit (you sit in a chair) is compared to the relationship between bed and what you do in it (you sleep in a bed). The missing word is bed.

Find the missing word in these analogies.

moon is to earth as earth is to ___sun___
tree is to lumber as wheat is to ___flour___
library is to books as kitchen is to ___utensils___
three is to six as four is to ___eight___
princess is to queen as prince is to ___king___
story is to read as song is to ___sing___
length is to weight as inches is to ___pounds___
blind is to deaf as see is to ___hear___
pen is to write as broom is to ___sweep___
wrist is to hand as ankle is to ___foot___
water is to ship as air is to ___plane___
engine is to go as brake is to ___stop___

©1995 Kelley Wingate Publications, Inc.   106   KW 1014

Name _____   skill: analogies

Analogies 4

Analogies compare relationships of words. For example:

chair is to sit as bed is to _____

The relationship of chair and sit (you sit in a chair) is compared to the relationship between bed and what you do in it (you sleep in a bed). The missing word is bed.

Find the missing word in these analogies.

glass is to break as paper is to ___cut___
soap is to clean as mud is to ___dirty___
silk is to smooth as sandpaper is to ___rough___
penny is to dollar as inch is to ___foot___
in is to out as hot is to ___cold___
frown is to angry as smile is to ___happy___
fat is to thin as dark is to ___light___
screwdriver is to hammer as screw is to ___nail___
cowboy is to cow as shepherd is to ___sheep___
cat is to kitten as dog is to ___puppy___
mother is to daughter as father is to ___son___
lawn is to grass as beach is to ___sand___

©1995 Kelley Wingate Publications, Inc.   107   KW 1014

Super Reader Award

_____

receives this award for

_____

Keep up the great work!

_____   _____
signed   date

Reading Award

_____

receives this award for

_____

Great Job!

_____   _____
signed   date

CD-3711

absorb	algae	analogy	armistice
armor	arrive	atmosphere	avoid
balance	barely	below	camouflage
carnivore	celebrate	character	chemicals

compare	comfortable	civil	choose
core	contrast	contest	consume
crisp	creek	crack	courage
describe	depend	declared	custom

eager	during	display	dishonor
fasting	express	erupt	earthquakes
gemstone	founder	feast	favorite
holiday	hiding	herbivore	glanced

liberty	independent	identify	host
miracle	message	mashed	magnet
observed	neighbors	mutualism	multiple
parade	ownership	orbits	omnivore

politics	perfect	pebbles	parasites
puddles	prefix	precious	power
relax	raised	radiate	pure
struggle	sediment	scavenger	riddles

suffix	surface	surrender	survive
symbolize	tablet	tangled	telescope
torch	transferred	twice	urn
victory	volcano	whipped	whisper